HTML
Pocket Reference

SECOND EDITION

HTML
Pocket Reference

Jennifer Niederst

O'REILLY®

Beijing · Cambridge · Farnham · Köln · Paris · Sebastopol · Taipei · Tokyo

HTML Pocket Reference, Second Edition

by Jennifer Niederst

Copyright © 2002, 2000 O'Reilly & Associates, Inc. All rights reserved.
Printed in the United States of America.

Published by O'Reilly & Associates, Inc., 1005 Gravenstein Highway North,
Sebastopol, CA 95472.

O'Reilly & Associates books may be purchased for educational,
business, or sales promotional use. Online editions are also available
for most titles (*safari.oreilly.com*). For more information contact our
corporate/institutional sales department: (800) 998-9938 or
corporate@oreilly.com.

Editor:	Lorrie LeJeune
Production Editor:	Jane Ellin
Cover Designer:	Hanna Dyer
Interior Designer:	Melanie Wang

Printing History:

January 2000:	First Edition.
January 2002:	Second Edition.

0-596-00296-3
[C]

Contents

HTML Pocket Reference

Introduction

This pocket reference provides a concise, yet thorough, listing of HTML tags and attributes specified by the W3C HTML 4.01 Specification, Netscape Navigator, and Internet Explorer.

Using This Book

The majority of this reference is an alphabetical listing of tags and their attributes with explanations and browser support information.

The "Tag Groups" section lists tags that are related in functionality, and "Tag Structures" provides examples of how standard web page elements are constructed.

At the end of the book are useful charts, including character entities and decimal to hexadecimal conversions.

For Further Reading

More in-depth explanations of HTML and web design can be found in O'Reilly & Associates' *Web Design in a Nutshell* by Jennifer Niederst and *HTML and XHTML: The Definitive Guide* by Chuck Musciano and Bill Kennedy. Also useful is *Webmaster in a Nutshell* by Stephen Spainhour and Robert Eckstein.

The browser support information in this book was provided by the HTML Compendium created by Ron Woodall. I encourage you to check out the Compendium's site (*http://www.htmlcompendium.org*) for extremely in-depth explanations of HTML tags, attributes, and values and the browsers that support them.

Conventions Used in This Book

The correct syntax appears to the right of each tag and indicates whether the tag is a container (with an end tag) or stands alone. Browser support information is indicated below each tag. Browsers that do not support the tag are shown in gray. Attribute support is indicated in italics in the attribute description.

Tag Groups

The following lists group HTML tags by similar function. See the "Alphabetical Tag List" section for complete descriptions of each tag.

Structural Tags

The following tags are used primarily to give the document structure.

```
<!DOCTYPE>
<base>
<body>
<head>
<html>
<link>
<meta>
<title>
```

Text Tags: Block-Level Elements

Block-level elements are always formatted with a line-break before and after, with most adding some amount of additional space above and below as well.

```
<address>
<blockquote>
<dd>
<div>
<dl>
<dt>
<h1> through <h6>
<li>
<ol>
<p>
<ul>
```

Text Tags: Inline Styles

The following tags affect the appearance of text. "Inline" means they can be applied to a string of characters within a block element without introducing line breaks.

```
<b>
<big>
<cite>
<code>
<em>
<font> (deprecated)
<i>
<kbd>
<pre>
<s> (deprecated)
<samp>
<small>
<span>
<strike> (deprecated)
```

```
<strong>
<sub>
<sup>
<tt>
<u> (deprecated)
<var>
```

Text Tags: Logical Styles

Logical or content-based styles describe the enclosed text's meaning, context, or usage and leave rendering of the tag to the browser.

```
<abbr>
<acronym>
<cite>
<code>
<del>
<div>
<em>
<ins>
<kbd>
<q>
<samp>
<span>
<strong>
<var>
```

Text Tags: Physical Styles

Physical styles provide specific display instructions.

```
<b>
<big>
<blink> (Navigator only)
<font> (deprecated)
<i>
<s> (deprecated)
<small>
```

```
<strike> (deprecated)
<sub>
<sup>
<tt>
<u> (deprecated)
```

List Tags

```
<dir> (deprecated)
<dl>
<dd>
<dt>
<li>
<menu> (deprecated)
<ol>
<ul>
```

Spacing and Positioning Tags

The following tags give authors control over the line breaks, alignment, and spacing within an HTML document.

```
<br>
<center> (deprecated)
<nobr> (nonstandard)
<pre>
<spacer>
<table> (<th>, <tr>, <td>)
<wbr> (nonstandard)
```

Linking Tags

The following tags are used to create links from one document to another.

```
<a>
<link> (most commonly used for style sheets)
<map> (used in client-side imagemaps)
<area> (used in client-side imagemaps)
```

Table Tags

The following tags are used in the creation and formatting of tables.

```
<caption>
<table>
<tr>
<td>
<th>
```

The following table structure tags are supported by HTML 4.01, Internet Explorer 4.0+, and Netscape 6.

```
<col>
<colgroup>
<tbody>
<thead>
<tfoot>
```

Frame Tags

Frames are created using the following tags.

```
<frame>
<frameset>
<noframes>
```

Form Tags

The following tags are used to define forms and their elements.

```
<button>
<form>
<input>
    (type=button|checkbox|file|hidden|image|
        password|radio|reset|submit|text)

<option>
<select>
<textarea>
```

The following form tags are supported by HTML 4.01, Internet Explorer 4.0+, and Netscape 6.

```
<fieldset>
<label>
<legend>
```

Multimedia Tags

The following tags are used to add multimedia elements to web pages.

```
<applet> (deprecated)
<bgsound> (Internet Explorer only)
<embed> (dropped from HTML 4)
<object>
<param>
```

Script Tags

The following tags are used to add scripts to HTML documents.

```
<script>
<noscript>
```

Deprecated Tags

The following tags have been deprecated in the HTML 4.01 specification, usually in favor of style sheet controls.

```
<applet>
<basefont>
<center>
<dir>
<font>
<isindex>
<menu>
<s>
<strike>
<u>
```

Navigator-only Tags

The following tags are supported only by Navigator.

```
<blink>
<ilayer>
<keygen>
<layer>
<multicol>
<server>
<spacer>
```

Internet Explorer-only Tags

The following tags are supported only by Internet Explorer.

```
<bgsound>
<comment>
<marquee>
<ruby>
<rt>
```

Tag Structures

The examples below show the tag structure for common web page elements. When an attribute appears in the tag, it indicates that the attribute is required.

HTML Document

The standard skeletal structure of an HTML document is as follows:

```
<HTML>
  <HEAD>
    <TITLE>document title</TITLE>
  </HEAD>
  <BODY>
    contents of document
  </BODY>
</HTML>
```

Lists

The following are examples of simple lists.

Definition list

```
<DL>
    <DT>
        <DD>
    <DT>
        <DD>
</DL>
```

Ordered (numbered) list

```
<OL>
    <LI>
    <LI>
    <LI>
</OL>
```

Unordered (bulleted) list

```
<UL>
    <LI>
    <LI>
    <LI>
</UL>
```

Nested list

```
<OL>
    <LI>
    <LI>
        <UL>
            <LI>
            <LI>
        </UL>
</OL>
```

Linking Within a Document

The first <a> tag specifies a named fragment; the second <a>
tag links back to that named fragment.

```
<A NAME="fragmentname">Text</A>
...
<A HREF="#fragmentname">Link to Text</A>
```

Client-Side Imagemap

In the example below, the image *graphic.gif* is an imagemap that contains two clickable areas and uses the client-side imagemap named *map1*.

```
<MAP NAME="map1">
        <AREA SHAPE="rect" COORDS="123,20,234,40"
        HREF="http://www.oreilly.com/">
        <AREA SHAPE="circ" COORDS="111,50,25"
        HREF="index.html">
</MAP>

<IMG SRC="graphic.gif" USEMAP="map1">
```

Basic Table

The following HTML sample shows the basic structure for a simple four-cell table. The number of columns is determined by the number of cells (<td>) that appear within each row (<tr>). The table in the example below has two rows and two columns.

```
<TABLE>
    <TR>
        <TD></TD>
        <TD></TD>
    </TR>
    <TR>
        <TD></TD>
        <TD></TD>
    </TR>
</TABLE>
```

Framed Document

The following code creates a framed document with two frames, side by side. The number of columns is established by the number of measurements listed in the cols attribute. To create a framed document with horizontal frames, use the ROWS attribute. For instance, <FRAMESET ROWS="*,*,*"> creates a framed document with three horizontal frames of equal height.

```
<HTML>
   <HEAD>
      <TITLE>Frame Document</TITLE>
   </HEAD>
   <FRAMESET COLS="*,*">
      <FRAME SRC="doc1.html">
      <FRAME SRC="doc2.html">
   </FRAMESET>
   <NOFRAMES>Your browser does not support frames.
   </NOFRAMES>
</HTML>
```

Nested frames

You can place one frameset within another as shown in the following example.

```
<FRAMESET COLS="*,*">
   <FRAME SRC="doc1.html">
   <FRAMESET ROWS="50,150">
      <FRAME SRC="doc2.html">
      <FRAME SRC="doc3.html">
</FRAMESET>
```

Adding Style Sheet Information

There are three methods for adding style sheet information to a document.

External style sheets:

```
<HEAD>
   <LINK rel="stylesheet" href="url of css file"
   type="text/css">
</HEAD>
```

Embedded style sheets:

```
<HEAD>
   <STYLE type="text/css">
   <!--
      selector {property: value}
```

```
    -->
    </STYLE>
</HEAD>
```

Inline styles (using the `style` attribute in an element tag):

```
<ELEMENT style="property: value">...</ELEMENT>
```

Example:
```
<H1 style="color: blue; font-size: 18pt;">...</H1>
```

Alphabetical Tag List

A number of attributes in the HTML 4.01 specification are shared by nearly all elements. To save space, they have been abbreviated in this book as they are in the specification as follows.

`%coreattrs` indicates the collection of core HTML attributes according to the HTML 4.01 specification:

id
> Assigns a unique identifying name to the element

class
> Assigns a classification name to the element

style
> Associated style information

title
> Advisory title/amplification

`%i18n` stands for "internationalization" (i + 18 characters + n) and includes attributes related to making documents and elements accessible in all languages:

lang
> Specifies the language for the element by its two-character language code

dir
> Specifies the direction of the element; values are `ltr` (left to right) or `rtl` (right to left)

%events indicates the core events (as defined in the HTML 4.01 Document Type Definition) used by scripting languages which are applicable to the element:

```
onclick, ondblclick, onmousedown, onmouseup,
onmouseover, onmousemove, onmouseout, onkeypress,
onkeydown, onkeyup
```

`<!--...-->`

`<!-->...</-->`

NN 2, 3, 4, 6   **MSIE** 2, 3, 4, 5, 5.5, 6   **HTML** 4.01   **WebTV**   **Opera5**

Identifies a comment. Text within comment tags will not be displayed by the browser.

`<!DOCTYPE>`

`<!DOCTYPE "DTD NAME">`

NN 2, 3, 4, 6   **MSIE** 2, 3, 4, 5, 5.5, 6   **HTML** 4.01   **WebTV**   **Opera5**

Specifies the document type definition that applies to the document.

Examples

```
<!DOCTYPE HTML PUBLIC "-//W3C//DTD HTML 4.01//EN">
<!DOCTYPE HTML PUBLIC "-//W3C//DTD HTML 4.01 Transitional/
/EN">
```

`<a>`

`<a>...</a>`

NN 2, 3, 4, 6   **MSIE** 2, 3, 4, 5, 5.5, 6   **HTML** 4.01   **WebTV**   **Opera5**

Defines an *anchor* within the document. An anchor is used to link to another document or web resource. It can also serve to label a fragment within a document (also called a *named anchor*), which serves as a destination anchor for linking to a specific point in an HTML document.

Attributes

The attributes labeled "HTML 4.01" are new to the HTML 4.01 specification and are generally supported only by Internet Explorer 5.5 and higher and Netscape 6.

%coreattrs, %i18n, %events, onfocus, onblur

accesskey=*character*
> HTML 4.01. Assigns an access key (shortcut key command) to the link. Access keys are also used for form fields. The value is a single character. Users may access the element by hitting Alt-*character* (PC) or Ctrl-*character* (Mac).

charset=*charset*
> HTML 4.01. Specifies the character encoding of the target document.

coords=*x,y coordinates*
> HTML 4.01. Specifies the x,y coordinates for a clickable area in an imagemap. HTML 4.0 proposes that client-side imagemaps be replaced by an <object> tag containing the image and a set of anchor tags defining the "hot" areas (with shapes and coordinate attributes). This system has not yet been implemented by browsers.

href=*url*
> Specifies the URL of the destination HTML document or web resource (such as an image, audio, PDF, or other media file).

hreflang=*language code*
> HTML 4.01. Specifies the base language of the target document.

id=*text*
> Gives the link a unique name (similar to the name attribute) so it can be referenced from a link, script, or style sheet. It is more versatile than name, but it is not as universally supported.

name=*text*
> Places a fragment identifier within an HTML document.

rel=*relationship*
> Establishes a relationship between the current document and the target document. Common relationships include stylesheet, next, prev, copyright, index, and glossary.

rev=*relationship*
> Specifies the relationship from the target back to the source (the opposite of the rev attribute).

`shape=rect|circle|poly|default`
> *HTML 4.01.* Defines the shape of a clickable area in an imagemap. This is only used in the `<a>` tag as part of HTML 4.01's proposal to replace client-side imagemaps with a combination of `<object>` and `<a>` tags. This system has not yet been implemented by browsers.

`tabindex=number`
> *HTML 4.01.* Specifies the position of the current element in the tabbing order for the current document. The value must be between 0 and 32,767. It is used for tabbing through the links on a page (or fields in a form).

`target=text`
> *Not supported by WebTV or Internet Explorer 2.0 and earlier.* Specifies the name of the window or frame in which the target document should be displayed.

`title=text`
> Specifies a title for the target document. May be displayed as a "tool tip."

`type=MIME type`
> Specifies the content type (MIME type) of the defined content.

Link Examples

To a local file:

```
<A HREF="filename.html">...</A>
```

To an external file:

```
<A HREF="http://server/path/file.html">...</A>
```

To a named anchor:

```
<A HREF="http://server/path/file.html#fragment">...</A>
```

To a named anchor in the current file:

```
<A HREF="#fragment">...</A>
```

To send an email message:

```
<A HREF="mailto:username@domain">...</A>
```

To a file on an FTP server:

```
<A HREF="ftp://server/path/filename">...</A>
```

`<abbr>`   `<abbr>...</abbr>`

NN 2, 3, 4, 6   **MSIE** 2, 3, 4, 5, **5.5, 6**   **HTML** 4.01   WebTV   **Opera5**

Identifies the enclosed text as an abbreviation. It has no inherent effect on text display but can be used as an element selector in a style sheet.

Attributes

%coreattrs, %i18n, %events

title=*text*
> Provides the full expression for the abbreviation. This may be useful for nonvisual browsers, speech synthesizers, translation systems, and search engines.

Example

```
<ABBR TITLE="Massachusetts">Mass.</ABBR>
```

`<acronym>`   `<acronym>...</acronym>`

NN 2, 3, 4, 6   **MSIE** 2, 3, **4, 5**, 5.5, 6   **HTML** 4.01   WebTV   **Opera5**

Indicates an acronym. It has no inherent effect on text display but can be used as an element selector in a style sheet.

Attributes

%coreattrs, %i18n, %events

title=*text*
> Provides the full expression for the acronym. This may be useful for nonvisual browsers, speech synthesizers, translation systems, and search engines.

Example

```
<ACRONYM TITLE="World Wide Web">WWW</ACRONYM>
```

<address>

<address>...</address>

NN 2, 3, 4, 6	MSIE 2, 3, 4, 5, 5.5, 6	HTML 4.01	WebTV	Opera5

Supplies the author's contact information, typically at the beginning or end of a document. Addresses are generally formatted in italic type with a line break (but no extra space) above and below.

Attributes

%coreattrs, %i18n, %events

<applet>

<applet>...</applet>

NN 2, 3, 4, 6	MSIE 2, 3, 4, 5, 5.5, 6	HTML 4.01	WebTV	Opera5

Deprecated. This tag (first introduced in Netscape Navigator 2.0) is used to place a Java applet on the web page. <applet> and all its attributes have been deprecated in favor of the <object> element, but it is still widely used. Some applets require the use of the <applet> tag. Furthermore, Navigator 4 and earlier and Internet Explorer 4 do not support Java applets via object tags.

Attributes

%coreattrs

align=left|right|top|middle|bottom
> Aligns the applet and allows text to wrap around it (same as image alignment).

alt=*text*
> Provides alternate text if the applet cannot be displayed.

archive=*urls*
> Provides a space-separated list of URLs with classes to be preloaded.

code=*class*
> *Required.* Specifies the class name of the code to be executed.

codebase=*url*
> URL from which the applet code is retrieved.

height=*number*
> *Required.* Height of the initial applet display area in pixels.

hspace=*number*

> Holds *number* pixels space clear to the left and right of the applet window.

name=*text*

> Names the applet for reference from elsewhere on the page.

object=*text*

> Names a resource containing a serialized representation of an applet's state. It is interpreted relative to the applet's code-base. The serialized data contains the applet's class name but not the implementation. The class name is used to retrieve the implementation from a class file or archive. Either code or object must be present. If both code and object are given, it is an error if they provide different class names.

vspace=*number*

> Holds *number* pixels space clear above and below the applet window.

width=*number*

> *Required.* Width of the initial applet display area in pixels.

`<area>` `<area>` *(no end tag)*

NN 2, 3, 4, 6	MSIE 2, 3, 4, 5, 5.5, 6	HTML 4.01	WebTV	Opera5

The area tag is used within the `<map>` tag of a *client-side imagemap* to define a specific "hot" (clickable) area.

Attributes

%coreattrs, %i18n, %events, onfocus, onblur

accesskey=*single character*

> Assigns an access key to the element. Pressing the access key gives focus to (jumps to and highlights) the element.

alt=*text*

> *Required.* Specifies a short description of the image that is displayed when the image file is not available.

coords=*values*

> Specifies a list of comma-separated pixel coordinates that define a "hot" area of an imagemap. The specific syntax for the coordinates varies by shape.

---

href=*url*
> Specifies the URL of the document or file that is accessed by clicking on the defined area.

nohref
> Defines a "mouse-sensitive" area in an imagemap for which there is no action when the user clicks in the area.

shape=rect|circle|poly|default
> Defines the shape of the clickable area.

tabindex=*number*
> Assigns the position of the current element in the tabbing order for the current document.

`<b>`
`<b>...</b>`

NN 2, 3, 4, 6   **MSIE** 2, 3, 4, 5, 5.5, 6   **HTML** 4.01   **WebTV**   **Opera5**

Enclosed text is rendered in bold.

Attributes

%coreattrs, %i18n, %events

`<base>`
`<base>` *(no end tag)*

NN 2, 3, 4, 6   **MSIE** 2, 3, 4, 5, 5.5, 6   **HTML** 4.01   **WebTV**   **Opera5**

Specifies the base pathname for all relative URLs in the document. Place this element within the `<head>` of the document.

Attributes

href=*url*
> *Required.* Specifies the URL to be used.

target=*name*
> *Not supported in MSIE 2.0.* Defines the default target window for all links in the document. Often used to target frames.

`<basefont>`

<basefont> *(no end tag)*

NN 2, 3, 4, 6   MSIE 2, 3, 4, 5, 5.5, 6   HTML 4.01   WebTV   Opera5

Deprecated. Specifies certain font attributes for text following the tag. It can be used within the `<head>` tags to apply to the entire document, or within the body of the document to apply to the subsequent text.

Attributes

size=*value*
> *Required.* Sets the basefont size using the HTML size values from 1 to 7 (or relative values based on the default value of 3). Subsequent relative size settings are based on this value.

Internet Explorer 3.0+ only

color="#*rrggbb*" *or name*
> Sets the color of the following text using hexadecimal RGB values.

face=*font*
> Sets the font for the following text.

`<bdo>`

<bdo>...</bdo>

NN 2, 3, 4, 6   MSIE 2, 3, 4, 5, 5.5, 6   HTML 4.01   WebTV   Opera5

Overrides the current directionality of the text ("bidirectional override").

Attributes

%coreattrs, %i18n

`<bgsound>`

<bgsound> *(no end tag)*

NN 2, 3, 4, 6   **MSIE 2, 3, 4, 5, 5.5, 6**   HTML 4.01   WebTV   Opera5

Internet Explorer only. Adds an audio file to the document to be used as a background sound when the page loads.

Attributes

`loop=number` or `infinite`
> Specifies the number of times the audio file plays.

`src=URL`
> *Required*. Specifies the location of the audio file.

<big>

<big>...</big>

NN 2, 3, 4, 6   **MSIE** 2, 3, 4, 5, 5.5, 6   **HTML** 4.01   **WebTV**   **Opera5**

Sets the type one font size increment larger than the surrounding text.

Attributes

%coreattrs, %i18n, %events

<blink>

<blink>...</blink>

NN 2, 3, 4, 6   MSIE 2, 3, 4, 5, 5.5, 6   HTML 4.01   WebTV   Opera5

Causes the contained text to flash on and off in Netscape browsers.

<blockquote>

<blockquote>...</blockquote>

NN 2, 3, 4, 6   **MSIE** 2, 3, 4, 5, 5.5, 6   **HTML** 4.01   **WebTV**   **Opera5**

Enclosed text is a "blockquote" (lengthy quotation), which is generally displayed with an indent on the left and right margins and added space above and below the paragraph.

Note that:

- Some older browsers display blockquote material in italic, making it difficult to read.

- Browsers are inconsistent in the way they display images within blockquotes. Some align the graphic with the indented blockquote margin; others align the image with the normal margin of paragraph text. It is a good idea to test on a variety of browsers.

Attributes

%coreattrs, %i18n, %events

cite=*URL*

> Provides information about the source from which the quotation was borrowed. Not often used.

`<body>` `<body>...</body>` *(start and end tags optional)*

NN 2, 3, 4, 6	MSIE 2, 3, 4, 5, 5.5, 6	HTML 4.01	WebTV	Opera5

Defines the beginning and the end of the document body. The body contains the content of the document (the part that is displayed in the browser window). Attributes to the `<body>` tag affect the entire document.

Attributes

%coreattrs, %i18n, %events

alink="#*rrggbb*" *or color name*

> *Deprecated.* Sets the color of active links (i.e., the color while the mouse button is held down during a "click"). Color is specified in hexadecimal RGB values or by standard web color name.

background=*url*

> *Deprecated.* Provides the URL to a graphic file to be used as a tiling graphic in the background of the document.

bgcolor="#*rrggbb*" *or color name*

> *Deprecated.* Sets the color of the background for the document. Color is specified in hexadecimal RGB values or by standard web color name.

link="#*rrggbb*" *or color name*

> *Deprecated.* Sets the default color for all the links in the document. Color is specified in hexadecimal RGB values or by standard web color name.

text="#*rrggbb*" *or color name*

> *Deprecated.* Sets the default color for all the non-hyperlink and unstyled text in the document. Color is specified in hexadecimal RGB values or by standard web color name.

vlink="#*rrggbb*" *or color name*
> *Deprecated.* Sets the color of the visited links (links that have already been followed) for the document. Color is specified in hexadecimal RGB values or by standard web color name.

Netscape Navigator 4.0+ only

marginwidth=*number*
> Specifies the distance (in number of pixels) between the left and right browser edges and the text and graphics in the window.

marginheight=*number*
> Specifies the distance (in number of pixels) between the top and bottom edges of the browser and the text or graphics in the window.

Internet Explorer only

bgproperties=fixed
> When this attribute is set to fixed, the background image does not scroll with the document content.

leftmargin=*number*
> Specifies the distance (in number of pixels) between the left browser edge and the beginning of the text and graphics in the window.

topmargin=*number*
> Specifies the distance (in number of pixels) between the top edge of the browser and the top edge of the text or graphics in the window.

rightmargin=*number*
> Specifies the distance (in number of pixels) between the right edge of the browser and the text or graphics in the window.

bottommargin=*number*
> Specifies the distance (in number of pixels) between the bottom edge of the browser and the bottom edge of the text or graphics in the window.

\

 (no end tag)

NN 2, 3, 4, 6	MSIE 2, 3, 4, 5, 5.5, 6	HTML 4.01	WebTV	Opera5

Breaks the text and begins a new line but does not add extra space.

Attributes

%coreattrs

clear=all|left|right|none
> Breaks the text flow and resumes the next line after the specified margin is clear. This is often used to start the text below an aligned image (preventing text wrap). none is the default, causing a simple line break.

\<button>

<button>...</button>

NN 2, 3, 4, 6	MSIE 2, 3, 4, 5.5, 6	HTML 4.01	WebTV	Opera5

Defines a "button" that functions similarly to buttons created with the input tag but allows for richer rendering possibilities. Buttons can contain content such as text and images (but not imagemaps).

Attributes

%coreattrs, %i18n, %events, onfocus, onblur

accesskey=*single character*
> Assigns an access key to the element. Pressing the access key gives focus to (jumps to and highlights) the element.

disabled
> Disables the form control for user input.

name=*text*
> *Required.* Assigns the control name for the element.

type=submit|reset|button
> Identifies the type of button: submit button (the default type), reset button, or custom button (used with JavaScript), respectively.

value=*text*

> Assigns the value to the button control. The behavior of the button is determined by the type attribute.

tabindex=*number*

> Assigns the position of the current element in the tabbing order for the current document.

<caption>

<caption>...</caption>

| NN 2, 3, 4, 6 | MSIE 2, 3, 4, 5, 5.5, 6 | HTML 4.01 | WebTV | Opera5 |

Provides a brief summary of the table's contents or purpose. The caption must immediately follow the <table> tag and precede all other tags. The width of the caption is determined by the width of the table. The caption's position as displayed in the browser can be controlled with the align attribute (or valign in MSIE).

Attributes

%coreattrs, %i18n, %events

align=top|bottom|left|right

> *Deprecated.* Positions the caption relative to the table. The default is top.

valign=top|bottom

> *Internet Explorer 3.0 and higher only.* Positions the caption above or below the table (top is the default).

<center>

<center>...</center>

| NN 2, 3, 4, 6 | MSIE 2, 3, 4, 5, 5.5, 6 | HTML 4.01 | WebTV | Opera5 |

Deprecated. Centers the enclosed elements horizontally on the page (a shortcut for <DIV align=center>).

Attributes

%coreattrs, %i18n, %events

<cite>

<cite>...</cite>

NN 2, 3, 4, 6   **MSIE** 2, 3, 4, 5, 5.5, 6   **HTML** 4.01   **WebTV**   **Opera5**

Denotes a citation—a reference to another document, especially a book, magazine, article, etc. Browsers generally display citations in italic.

Attributes

%coreattrs, %i18n, %events

<code>

<code>...</code>

NN 2, 3, 4, 6   **MSIE** 2, 3, 4, 5, 5.5, 6   **HTML** 4.01   **WebTV**   **Opera5**

Denotes a code sample. Code is rendered in the browser's specified monospace font (usually Courier).

Attributes

%coreattrs, %i18n, %events

<col>

<col> (no end tag)

NN 2, 3, 4, 6   **MSIE** 2, 3, 4, 5, 5.5, 6   **HTML** 4.01   WebTV   Opera5

Specifies properties for a column (or group of columns) within a *column group* (<colgroup>). Columns can share attributes (such as text alignment) without being part of a formal structural grouping.

Column groups and columns were introduced by Internet Explorer 3.0 and are now proposed by the HTML 4.01 specification as a standard way to label table structure. They may also be useful in speeding table display (i.e., the columns can be displayed incrementally without waiting for the entire contents of the table).

Attributes

%coreattrs, %i18n, %events

align=left|right|center|justify|char
> *Deprecated.* Specifies alignment of text in the cells of a column. The default value is left.

char=character
> Specifies a character along which the cell contents will be aligned when align is set to char. The default character is a decimal point (language-appropriate). This attribute is generally not supported by current browsers.

charoff=length
> Specifies the offset distance to the first alignment character (char) on each line. If a line doesn't use an alignment character, it should be horizontally shifted to end at the alignment position. This attribute is generally not supported by current browsers.

span=number
> Specifies the number of columns "spanned" by the <col> element. The default value is 1. All columns indicated in the span are formatted according to the attribute settings in <col>.

valign=top|middle|bottom|baseline
> *Deprecated.* Specifies the vertical alignment of text in the cells of a column.

width=pixels, percentage, n*
> Specifies the width of each column spanned by the <col> element. Width can be measured in pixels or percentages, or defined as a relative size (*). For example, 2* sets the column two times wider than the other columns; 0* sets the column width at the minimum necessary to hold the column's contents. width in the <col> tag overrides the width settings of the containing <colgroup> element.

\<colgroup\>   <colgroup>...</colgroup> *(end tag optional)*

NN 2, 3, 4, **6**   **MSIE** 2, **3, 4, 5, 5.5, 6**   **HTML** **4.01**   WebTV   Opera5

Creates a *column group*, a structural division within a table that can be appointed attributes with style sheets or HTML. A table may include more than one column group. The number of columns in a group is specified either by the value of the span attribute or by a tally of columns <col> within the group. Its end tag is optional.

Column groups and columns were introduced by Internet Explorer 3.0 and are now proposed by the HTML 4.0

specification as a standard way to label table structure. They may also be useful in speeding the table display (i.e., the columns can be displayed incrementally without waiting for the entire contents of the table).

Attributes

%coreattrs, %i18n, %events

align=left|right|center|justify|char
> *Deprecated.* Specifies the alignment of text in the cells of a column group. The default value is left.

char=*character*
> Specifies a character along which the cell contents will be aligned when align is set to char. The default character is a decimal point (language-appropriate). This attribute is generally not supported by current browsers.

charoff=*length*
> Specifies the distance to the first alignment character (char) on each line. If a line doesn't use an alignment character, it should be horizontally shifted to end at the alignment position. This attribute is generally not supported by current browsers.

span=*number*
> Specifies the number of columns in a column group. If span is not specified, the default is 1.

valign=top|middle|bottom|baseline
> *Deprecated.* Specifies the vertical alignment of text in the cells of a column group. The default is middle.

width=*pixels, percentage, n**
> Specifies a default width for each column in the current column group. Width can be measured in pixels, percentages, or defined as a relative size (*). 0* sets the column width at the minimum necessary to hold the column's contents.

\<comment\> \<comment\>...\</comment\>

NN 2, 3, 4, 6	**MSIE** 2, 3, **4, 5, 5.5, 6**	HTML 4.01	**WebTV**	Opera5

Indicates a comment in Internet Explorer and WebTV. Comments are not displayed in the browser.

`<dd>`

<dd>...</dd> *(end tag optional)*

NN 2, 3, 4, 6   **MSIE** 2, 3, 4, 5, 5.5, 6   **HTML** 4.01   **WebTV**   **Opera5**

Denotes the definition portion of an item within a definition list. The definition is usually displayed with an indented left margin. The closing tag is commonly omitted but should be included when applying style sheets.

Attributes

%coreattrs, %i18n, %events

compact
> *Deprecated.* Makes the list as small as possible. Few browsers support the compact attribute.

`<del>`

<del>...</del>

NN 2, 3, 4, 6   **MSIE** 2, 3, 4, 5, 5.5, 6   **HTML** 4.01   WebTV   **Opera5**

Indicates deleted text. It has no inherent style qualities on its own but may be used to hide deleted text from view or display it as strike-through text via style sheet controls. It may be useful for legal documents and any instance where edits need to be tracked. Its counterpart is *inserted* text (<ins>). Both can be used to indicate either inline or block-level elements.

Attributes

%coreattrs, %i18n, %events

cite=*URL*
> Can be set to point to a source document that explains why the document was changed.

datetime=*YYYY-MM-DDThh:mm:ssTZD*
> Specifies the date and time the change was made. Dates and times follow the format listed above where YYYY is the four-digit year, MM is the two-digit month, DD is the day, hh is the hour (00 through 23), mm is the minute (00 through 59), and ss is the seconds (00 through 59). The TZD stands for "Time Zone Designator" and its value can be Z (to indicate UTC, Coordinated Universal Time), an indication of the number of hours and minutes ahead of UTC (such as +03:00); or an

indication of the number of hours and minutes behind UTC (such as –02:20).

This is the standard format for date and time values in HTML. For more information, see *http://www.w3.org/TR/1998/NOTE-datetime-19980827*.

\<dfn\>

\<dfn\>...\</dfn\>

NN 2, 3, 4, 6	MSIE 2, 3, 4, 5, 5.5, 6	HTML 4.01	WebTV	Opera5

Indicates the defining instance of the enclosed term. Usually rendered in bold text, it calls attention to the introduction of special terms and phrases.

Attributes

%coreattrs, %i18n, %events

\<dir\>

\<dir\>...\</dir\>

NN 2, 3, 4, 6	MSIE 2, 3, 4, 5, 5.5, 6	HTML 4.01	WebTV	Opera5

Deprecated. Creates a directory list consisting of list items \<li\>. Directory lists were originally designed to display lists of files with short names, but they have been deprecated with the recommendation that unordered lists (\<ul\>) be used instead. Most browsers render directory lists as they do unordered lists (with bullets), although some use a multicolumn format.

Attributes

%coreattrs, %i18n, %events

compact
> *Deprecated.* Makes the list as small as possible. Few browsers support the compact attribute.

\<div\>

\<div\>...\</div\>

NN 2, 3, 4, 6	MSIE 2, 3, 4, 5, 5.5, 6	HTML 4.01	WebTV	Opera5

Denotes a generic "division" within the document. This element can be used to add structure to an HTML document. When \<div\>

---

was first introduced in HTML 3.2, only the alignment function (using the `align` attribute) was implemented by the major browsers. While it has no presentation properties of its own, it can be used in conjunction with the `class` and `id` attributes and then formatted with style sheets. Because divisions are block elements, they usually display with some added space above and below.

Attributes

%coreattrs, %i18n, %events

align=center|left|right
> *Deprecated.* Aligns the text within the tags to the left, right, or center of the page.

class=*name*
> Assigns a name to an element or a number of elements. Elements that share a class identification can be treated as a group.

id=*name*
> Assigns a unique name to an element. There can not be two elements with the same `id` name in a document.

style=*style properties*
> Embeds formatting information to be applied to the division contents.

`<dl>`   `<dl>...</dl>`

NN 2, 3, 4, 6	MSIE 2, 3, 4, 5, 5.5, 6	HTML 4.01	WebTV	Opera5

Indicates a definition list, consisting of terms (`<dt>`) and definitions (`<dd>`).

Attributes

%coreattrs, %i18n, %events

compact
> *Deprecated.* Makes the list as small as possible. Few browsers support the `compact` attribute.

<dt>

<dt>...</dt> *(end tag optional)*

| NN 2, 3, 4, 6 | MSIE 2, 3, 4, 5, 5.5, 6 | HTML 4.01 | WebTV | Opera5 |

Denotes the term portion of an item within a definition list. The closing tag is normally omitted but should be included when applying style sheets.

Attributes

%coreattrs, %i18n, %events

<em>

<em>...</em>

| NN 2, 3, 4, 6 | MSIE 2, 3, 4, 5, 5.5, 6 | HTML 4.01 | WebTV | Opera5 |

Indicates emphasized text. Nearly all browsers render emphasized text in italic.

Attributes

%coreattrs, %i18n, %events

<embed>

<embed>...</embed>

| NN 2, 3, 4, 6 | MSIE 2, 3, 4, 5, 5.5, 6 | HTML 4.01 | WebTV | Opera5 |

Embeds an object into the web page. Embedded objects are most often multimedia files that require special plug-ins to display (for example, Flash movies, Quicktime movies, etc.). In addition to the standard attributes listed below, certain media types and their respective plug-ins may have additional proprietary attributes for controlling the playback of the file. The closing tag is not always required, but is recommended.

Attributes

align=left|right|top|bottom
> *NN 4.0+ and MSIE 4.0+ only.* Controls the alignment of the media object relative to the surrounding text. The default is bottom. top and bottom are vertical alignments. left and right position the object on the left or right margin and allow text to wrap around it.

height=*number*

> Specifies the height of the object in number of pixels. Some media types require this attribute.

hidden=yes|no

> Hides the media file or player from view when set to yes. The default is no.

name=*name*

> Specifies a name for the embedded object. This is particularly useful for referencing the object from a script.

palette=foreground|background

> *NN 4.0+ and MSIE 4.0+ only.* This attribute applies to the Windows platform only. A value of foreground makes the plug-in's palette the foreground palette. Conversely, a value of background makes the plug-in use the background palette; this is the default.

pluginspage=*url*

> *NN 4.0+ and MSIE 4.0+ only.* Specifies the URL for information on installing the appropriate plug-in.

src=*url*

> *Required.* Provides the URL to the file or object to be placed on the page.

width=*number*

> Specifies the width of the object in number of pixels. Some media types require this attribute.

Internet Explorer only

alt=*text*

> Provides alternative text when the media object cannot be displayed (same as for the <img> tag).

code=*filename*

> Specifies the class name of the Java code to be executed.

codebase=*url*

> Specifies the base URL for the application.

`units=pixels|en`

> Defines the measurement units used by height and width. The default is pixels. En units are half the point size of the body text.

Netscape Navigator only

`border=number`

> Specifies the width of the border (in pixels) around the media object.

`frameborder=yes|no`

> Turns the border on or off.

`hspace=number`

> Used in conjunction with the align attribute, the horizontal space attribute specifies (in pixels) the amount of space to leave clear to the left and right of the media object.

`pluginurl=url`

> Specifies a source for installing the appropriate plug-in for the media file. Netscape recommends that you use pluginurl instead of pluginspage.

`type=MIME type`

> Specifies the MIME type of the plug-in needed to run the file. Navigator uses either the value of the type attribute or the suffix of the filename given as the source to determine which plug-in to use.

`vspace=number`

> Used in conjunction with the align attribute, the vertical space attribute specifies (in pixels) the amount of space to leave clear above and below the media object.

<fieldset>   <fieldset>...</fieldset>

NN 2, 3, 4, 6   **MSIE** 2, 3, 4, 5.5, 6   **HTML** 4.01   WebTV   **Opera5**

Used to encapsulate a section of forms content, creating a group of related form fields. The proper use of this tag should make documents more accessible to nonvisual browsers. It is similar to <div> but is specifically for grouping fields. It was introduced to improve form accessibility to users with alternative browsing devices.

Attributes

%coreattrs, %i18n, %events

<font>

<font>...</font>

NN 2, 3, 4, 6	MSIE 2, 3, 4, 5, 5.5, 6	HTML 4.01	WebTV	Opera5

Deprecated. Used to affect the style (color, typeface, and size) of the enclosed text.

Attributes

%coreattrs, %i18n

color=*color name or #RRGGBB*
: *Deprecated.* Specifies the color of the enclosed text.

face=*typeface (or list of typefaces)*
: *Deprecated.* Specifies a typeface for the text. The specified typeface is used only if it is found on the user's machine. You may provide a list of fonts (separated by commas), and the browser uses the first available in the string.

size=*value*
: *Deprecated.* Sets the size of the type to an absolute value on a scale from 1 to 7 (3 is the default), or using a relative value *+n* or *-n* (based on the default or <basefont> setting).

<form>

<form>...</form>

NN 2, 3, 4, 6	MSIE 2, 3, 4, 5.5, 6	HTML 4.01	WebTV	Opera5

Indicates the beginning and end of a form. There can be more than one form in an HTML document, but forms cannot be nested inside one another, and it is important that they do not overlap.

Attributes

%coreattrs, %i18n, %events, onsubmit, onreset

accept=*content-type-list*
: Specifies a comma-separated list of file types (MIME types) that the server will accept and is able to process. Browsers

may one day be able to filter out unacceptable files when prompting a user to upload files to the server, but this attribute is not yet widely supported.

`accept-charset=charset list`

Specifies the list of character encodings for input data that must be accepted by the server in order to process the current form. The value is a space- and/or comma-delimited list of ISO character set names. The default value is unknown. This attribute is not widely supported.

`action=url`

Required. Specifies the URL of the application that will process the form. The default is the current URL.

`enctype=encoding`

Specifies how the values for the form controls are encoded when they are submitted to the server when the method is post. The default is the Internet Media Type (application/x-www-form-urlencoded). The value multipart/form-data should be used in combination with the file input element.

`method=get|post`

Specifies which HTTP method will be used to submit the form data. With get (the default), the information is appended to and sent along with the URL itself.

`name=text`

Names the element so that it may be referred to from style sheets or scripts

`target=name`

Specifies a target for the results of the form submission to be loaded so results can be displayed in another window or frame. The special target values _bottom, _top, _parent, and _self may be used.

`<frame>`

`<frame>` *(no end tag)*

NN 2, 3, 4, 6	MSIE 2, 3, 4, 5, 5.5, 6	HTML 4.01	WebTV	Opera5

Defines a single frame within a `<frameset>`.

Attributes

`%coreattrs`

bordercolor="#rrggbb" *or color name*
> *Nonstandard.* Sets the color for the frame's borders (if the border is turned on). Support for this attribute is limited to Netscape Navigator 3.0+ and Internet Explorer 4.0+.

frameborder=1|0 *(IE 3+ and W3C 4.0 Spec.);* yes|no *(NN 3+ and IE 4.0+)*
> Determines whether there is a 3D separator drawn between the current frame and surrounding frames. A value of 1 (or yes) turns the border on. A value of 0 (or no) turns the border off. The default value is 1 (border on). You may also set the frameborder at the frameset level, which may be more reliable.
>
> Because Netscape and Internet Explorer support different values, you need to specify the frameborder twice within <frame> to ensure full browser compatibility, as follows:
>
>   frameborder=yes frameborder=1 ...

longdesc=*url*
> Specifies a link to a document containing a long description of the frame and its contents. This addition to the HTML 4.01 specification may be useful for nonvisual web browsers, but it is currently not well supported.

marginwidth=*number*
> Specifies the amount of space (in pixels) between the left and right edges of the frame and its contents. The minimum value according to the HTML specification is 1 pixel. Setting the value to 0 in order to place objects flush against the edge of the frame works in Internet Explorer, but Netscape will still display a 1-pixel margin space.

marginheight=*number*
> Specifies the amount of space (in pixels) between the top and bottom edges of the frame and its contents. The minimum value according to the HTML specification is 1 pixel. Setting the value to 0 in order to place objects flush against the edge of the frame works in Internet Explorer, but Netscape will still display a 1-pixel margin space.

name=*text*
> Assigns a name to the frame. This name may be referenced by targets within links to make the target document load within the named frame.

`noresize`

> Prevents users from resizing the frame. By default, despite specific frame size settings, users can resize a frame by clicking and dragging its borders.

`scrolling=yes|no|auto`

> Specifies whether scrollbars appear in the frame. A value of yes means scrollbars always appear; a value of no means scrollbars never appear; a value of auto (the default) means scrollbars appear automatically when the contents do not fit within the frame.

`src=url`

> Specifies the location of the initial HTML file to be displayed by the frame.

`<frameset>`   `<frameset>...</frameset>`

NN 2, 3, 4, 6   **MSIE** 2, 3, 4, 5, 5.5, 6   **HTML** 4.01   **WebTV**   **Opera5**

Defines a collection of frames or other framesets.

Attributes

`%coreattrs, onload, unload`

`border=number`

> *Nonstandard.* Sets frame border thickness (in pixels) between all the frames in a frameset (when the frame border is turned on).

`bordercolor="#rrggbb"` *or color name*

> *Nonstandard.* Sets a border color for all the borders in a frameset. Support for this attribute is limited to Netscape Navigator 3.0 and higher and Internet Explorer 4.0.

`cols=list of lengths (number, percentage, or *)`

> Establishes the number and sizes of columns (vertical frames) in a frameset. The number of columns is determined by the number of values in the list. Size specifications can be in absolute pixel values, percentage values, or relative values (*) based on available space.

`frameborder=1|0` *(IE 3+)*; `yes|no` *(NN 3+ and IE 4.0+)*
> *Nonstandard.* Determines whether 3D separators are drawn between frames in the frameset. A value of 1 (or yes) turns the borders on; 0 (or no) turns the borders off.
>
> Because Netscape and Internet Explorer support different values, you may need to specify the frameborder twice within `<frameset>` to ensure cross-browser compatibility, as follows:
>
> ```
> frameborder=yes frameborder=1 ...
> ```

`framespacing=number` *(IE only)*
> *Internet 3.0 and higher only.* Adds additional space (in pixels) between adjacent frames.

`rows=list of lengths (number, percentage, or *)`
> Establishes the number and size of rows (horizontal frames) in the frameset. The number of rows is determined by the number of values in the list. Size specifications can be in absolute pixel values, percentage values, or relative values (*) based on available space.

`<h1>` through `<h6>`   `<hn>...</hn>`

NN 2, 3, 4, 6	MSIE 2, 3, 4, 5, 5.5, 6	HTML 4.01	WebTV	Opera5

Specifies that the enclosed text is a heading (a brief description of the section it introduces). There are six different levels of headings, from `<h1>` to `<h6>`, with `<h1>` the largest and each subsequent level displaying at a smaller size. `<h5>` and `<h6>` usually display smaller than the surrounding body text.

Attributes

`%coreattrs, %i18n, %events`

`align=center|left|right`
> *Deprecated.* Used to align the header left, right, or centered on the page. Microsoft Internet Explorer 3.0 and earlier do not support right alignment.

`<head>`

`<head>`...`</head>` *(start and end tags optional)*

NN 2, 3, 4, 6   **MSIE** 2, 3, 4, 5, 5.5, 6   **HTML** 4.01   **WebTV**   **Opera5**

Defines the head (also called "header") portion of the document that contains information about the document. The `<head>` tag has no directly displayed content, but serves only as a container for the other header tags, such as `<base>`, `<meta>`, and `<title>`.

Attributes

%i18n

profile=*URL*
> Provides the location of a predefined metadata profile that can be referenced by `<meta>` tags in the `<head>` of the document. This attribute is not yet implemented by browsers.

`<hr>`

`<hr>` *(no end tag)*

NN 2, 3, 4, 6   **MSIE** 2, 3, 4, 5, 5.5, 6   **HTML** 4.01   **WebTV**   **Opera5**

Adds a horizontal rule to the page.

Attributes

%coreattrs, %i18n, %events

align=center|left|right
> *Deprecated.* If the rule is shorter than the width of the window, this tag controls horizontal alignment of the rule. The default is center.

noshade
> *Deprecated.* This displays the rule as a solid (non-shaded) bar.

size=*number*
> *Deprecated.* Specifies the thickness of the rule in pixels.

width=*number or %*
> *Deprecated.* Specifies the length of the rule in pixels or as a percentage of the page width. By default, rules are the full width of the browser window.

\<html\>

<html>...</html> *(start and end tags optional)*

NN 2, 3, 4, 6   **MSIE** 2, 3, 4, 5, 5.5, 6   **HTML** 4.01   **WebTV**   **Opera5**

Placed at the beginning and end of the document, this tag tells the browser that the entire document is composed in HTML.

Attributes

dir=ltr|rtl

Indicates the direction the text should be rendered by the browser. The default is ltr (left-to-right), but some languages require rtl (right-to-left) rendering. The lang and dir attributes are part of the internationalization efforts incorporated into the HTML 4.01 specification. They can be added to almost any HTML element, but their use in the <html> tag is common for establishing the language for a whole document.

lang=*language code*

Indicates the primary language of the document.

version="-//W3C//DTD HTML 4.01//EN"

Deprecated. Specifies the version of HTML the document uses (the value above specifies 4.01). It has been deprecated in favor of the SGML <!DOCTYPE> declaration placed before the <html> tag.

\<i\>

...

NN 2, 3, 4, 6   **MSIE** 2, 3, 4, 5, 5.5, 6   **HTML** 4.01   **WebTV**   **Opera5**

Enclosed text is displayed in italic.

Attributes

%coreattrs, %i18n, %events

\<iframe\>

<iframe>...</iframe>

NN 2, 3, 4, 6   **MSIE** 2, 3, 4, 5, 5.5, 6   **HTML** 4.01   **WebTV**   **Opera5**

Defines an inline (floating) frame within a document with similar placement tags to <img>. This element requires a closing tag. Any content contained within the <iframe> tags will display on browsers that do not support inline frames.

Attributes

%coreattrs, %i18n, %events

align=top|middle|bottom|left|right
> Aligns the inline frame on the page within the flow of the text. Left and right alignment allows text to flow around the inline frame.

frameborder=1|0
> Turns on or off the displaying of a 3D border for the inline frame. The default is 1, which displays the border.

height=*number*
> Specifies the height of the inline frame in pixels or as a percentage of the window size. Internet Explorer and Navigator use a default height of 150 pixels.

hspace=*number*
> *Nonstandard.* Used in conjunction with left and right alignment, this attribute specifies the amount of space (in pixels) to hold clear to the left and right of the inline frame.

longdesc=*url*
> Specifies a link to a document containing a long description of the inline frame and its contents. This addition to the HTML 4.01 specification may be useful for nonvisual web browsers.

marginheight=*number*
> Specifies the amount of space (in pixels) between the top and bottom edges of the inline frame and its contents.

marginwidth=*number*
> Specifies the amount of space (in pixels) between the left and right edges of the inline frame and its contents.

name=*text*
> Assigns a name to the inline frame to be referenced by targeted links.

noresize=*number*
> *Nonstandard.* Prevents a frame from being resized by the user.

scrolling=yes|no|auto
> Determines whether scrollbars appear in the inline frame (see the earlier explanation of this attribute in <frame>).

src=*url*
> Specifies the URL of the HTML document to display initially in the inline frame.

vspace=*number*
> *Nonstandard.* Used in conjunction with left and right alignment, this attribute specifies the amount of space (in pixels) to hold clear above and below the inline frame.

width=*number*
> Specifies the width of the inline frame in pixels or as a percentage of the window size. Internet Explorer and Navigator use a default width of 300 pixels.

<ilayer>   <ilayer>...</ilayer>

NN 2, 3, 4, 6   **MSIE** 2, 3, 4, 5, 5.5, 6   **HTML** 4.01   **WebTV**   **Opera5**

Identifies an inflow layer in Navigator versions 4 through 4.7. Inflow layers appear in the flow of the document, as opposed to a general layer (<layer>), which can be positioned absolutely regardless of its position in the document. Netscape abandoned the <layer> and <ilayer> elements in Netscape 6 in favor of the standards-compliant <div> tag for similar functionality.

Attributes

See the <layer> entry for list of supported attributes.

<img>   <img> *(no end tag)*

NN 2, 3, 4, 6   **MSIE** 2, 3, 4, 5, 5.5, 6   **HTML** 4.01   **WebTV**   **Opera5**

Places a graphic on the page.

Attributes

align=*type*
> *Deprecated.* Specifies the alignment of an image using one of the following attributes:

Type	Resulting alignment
absbottom	*Navigator 3.0 + and Internet Explorer 4.0 + only.* Aligns the bottom of the image with the bottom of the current line.
absmiddle	*Navigator 3.0 + and Internet Explorer 4.0 + only.* Aligns the middle of the image with the middle of the current line.
baseline	*Navigator 3.0 + and Internet Explorer 4.0 + only.* Aligns the bottom of the image with the baseline of the current line.
bottom	Aligns the bottom of the image with the text baseline. This is the default vertical alignment.
center	According to the W3C specification, this centers the image horizontally on the page; however, in practice, browsers treat it the same as align=middle.
left	Aligns the image on the left margin and allows subsequent text to wrap around it.
middle	Aligns the text baseline with the middle of the image.
right	Aligns the image on the right margin and allows subsequent text to wrap around it.
texttop	*Navigator only.* Aligns the top of the image with the ascenders of the text line. An ascender is the part of a lowercase letter (like "d") that rises above the main body of the letter.
top	Aligns the top of the image with the top of the tallest object on that line.

alt=*text*

> *Required.* Provides a string of alternative text that appears when the image is not displayed. Internet Explorer 4.0+ and Netscape 6 on Windows display this text as a "tool tip" when the mouse rests on the image.

border=*number*

> Specifies the width (in pixels) of the border that surrounds a linked image. It is standard practice to set **border**=0 to turn the border off.

height=*number*

> Specifies the height of the image in pixels. It is not required, but is recommended to speed up the rendering of the web page.

hspace=*number*

> Specifies (in number of pixels) the amount of space to leave clear to the left and right of the image.

ismap

> Indicates that the graphic is used as the basis for a server-side imagemap (an image containing multiple hypertext links). See Chapter 11 for more information on server-side imagemaps.

longdesc=*url*

> Specifies a link to a long description of the image or an imagemap's contents. This may one day be used to make information about the image accessible to nonvisual browsers, but it is not currently supported.

lowsrc=*url*

> *Netscape Navigator (all versions) and Internet Explorer 4.0+ only.* Specifies an image (usually of a smaller file size) that will download first, followed by the final image specified by the **src** attribute.

name=*text*

> Assigns the image element a name so it can be referred to by a script or style sheet.

src=*url*

> *Required.* Provides the location of the graphic file to be displayed.

usemap=*url*

> Specifies the map containing coordinates and links for a client-side imagemap (an image containing multiple hypertext links). See Chapter 11 for more information on client-side imagemaps.

vspace=*number*

> Specifies (in number of pixels) the amount of space to leave clear above and below the image.

width=*number*

> Specifies the width of the image in pixels. It is not required, but is recommended to speed up the rendering of the web page.

Internet Explorer's dynsrc attribute

Using a `dynsrc` attribute, Internet Explorer Versions 2.0 and later also use the `<img>` tag to place a video on the page. The following attributes are related to the `dynsrc` function and work only with Internet Explorer:

controls
> Displays playback controls for the video.

dynsrc=*url*
> Provides the location of the video file to be displayed on the page.

loop=*number*|infinite
> Sets the number of times to play the video. It can be a number value or set to `infinite`.

start=fileopen|mouseover|fileopen, mouseover
> Specifies when to play the video. By default, it begins playing as soon as it's downloaded (`fileopen`). You can set it to start when the mouse pointer is over the movie area (`mouseover`). If you combine them (separated by a comma), the movie plays once when it's downloaded, then again every time the user mouses over it.

`<input type=button>`   `<input type=button>` *(no end tag)*

NN 2, 3, 4, 6   **MSIE** 2, 3, 4, 5.5, 6   **HTML** 4.01   **WebTV**   **Opera5**

Creates a customizable "push" button. Customizable buttons have no specific behavior but can be used to trigger functions created with JavaScript controls. Data from `type=button` controls is never sent with a form when a form is submitted to the server; these button controls are only for use with script programs on the browser.

Attributes

%coreattrs, %i18n, %events, onblur, onfocus, onselect, onchange

name=*string*
> *Required.* Assigns a name to the push button control. A script program uses this name to reference this control.

---

value=*string*
> *Required.* Specifies the value for this control.

<input type=checkbox>   `<input type=checkbox>` *(no end tag)*

NN 2, 3, 4, 6   **MSIE 2, 3, 4, 5.5, 6**   **HTML4.0**   **WebTV**   **Opera5**

Creates a checkbox input element within a `<form>`. Checkboxes are like on/off switches that can be toggled by the user. Several checkboxes in a group may be selected at one time. When a form is submitted, only the "on" checkboxes submit values to the server.

Attributes

%coreattrs, %i18n, %events, onblur, onfocus, onselect, onchange

checked
> When this attribute is added, the checkbox will be checked by default.

name=*text*
> *Required.* Assigns a name to the checkbox to be passed to the form-processing application if selected. Giving several checkboxes the same name creates a group of checkbox elements, allowing users to select several options with the same property.

value=*text*
> *Required.* Specifies the value of this control; this value is passed to the server only if the checkbox is selected. If no value is set, a default value of on is sent.

<input type=file>   `<input type=file>` *(no end tag)*

NN 2, 3, 4, 6   **MSIE 2, 3, 4, 5.5, 6**   **HTML 4.01**   **WebTV**   **Opera5**

Allows users to submit external files with their form submission. It is accompanied by a "browse" button when displayed in the browser.

Attributes

%coreattrs, %i18n, %events, onblur, onfocus, onselect, onchange

accept=*MIME type*
> Specifies a comma-separated list of content types that a server processing the form will handle correctly. It can be used to filter out nonconforming files when prompting a user to select files to send to the server.

name=*text*
> *Required.* Assigns a name to the control.

\<input type=hidden\>   \<input type=hidden\> *(no end tag)*

NN 2, 3, 4, 6   MSIE 2, 3, 4, 5.5, 6   HTML 4.01   WebTV   Opera5

Creates an element that does not display in the browser. Hidden controls can be used to pass special form-processing information to the server that the user cannot see or alter.

Attributes

%coreattrs, %i18n, %events, onblur, onfocus, onselect, onchange

name=*text*
> *Required.* Specifies the name of the control; this name (and the corresponding value) are passed to the form-processing application.

value=*text*
> *Required.* Specifies the value of the element that is passed to the form-processing application.

\<input type=image\>   \<input type=image\> *(no end tag)*

NN 2, 3, 4, 6   MSIE 2, 3, 4, 5.5, 6   HTML 4.01   WebTV   Opera5

Allows an image to be used as a substitute for a submit button. If a type=image button is pressed, the form is submitted.

Attributes

%coreattrs, %i18n, %events, onblur, onfocus, onselect,
onchange

align=top|middle|bottom
> Aligns the image with respect to the surrounding text lines.

alt=*text*
> Provides a text description if the image can not be seen.

name=*text*
> *Required.* Specifies the name of the control; this name (and the corresponding value) are passed to the form-processing application, along with data giving the coordinates of the mouse on top of the control image.

src=*url*
> *Required.* Provides the URL of the image.

\<input type=password\>   \<input type=password\> *(no end tag)*

NN 2, 3, 4, 6   **MSIE 2, 3, 4, 5.5, 6**   **HTML 4.01**   **WebTV**   **Opera5**

Creates a text-input element (like \<input type=text\>), but the input text is rendered in a way that hides the characters, such as by displaying a string of asterisks (*) or bullets (•). Note that this does *not* encrypt the information entered and should not be considered a real security measure.

Attributes

%coreattrs, %i18n, %events, onblur, onfocus, onselect,
onchange

maxlength=*number*
> Specifies the maximum number of characters the user can input for this element. The default is an unlimited number of characters.

name=*text*
> *Required.* Specifies the name of this control to be passed to the form-processing application for this element.

---

size=number
> Specifies the size of the text-entry box (measured in number of characters) to be displayed for this element. Users can type entries that are longer than the space provided, causing the field to scroll to the right.

value=text
> *Required.* Specifies the value that will initially be displayed in the text box.

`<input type=radio>`   `<input type=radio>` *(no end tag)*

NN 2, 3, 4, 6   **MSIE** 2, 3, 4, 5.5, 6   **HTML** 4.01   **WebTV**   **Opera5**

Creates a radio button that can be turned on and off. When a group of radio buttons shares the same control name, only one button within the group can be "on" at one time, and all the others are "off." This makes them different from checkboxes, which allow multiple choices to be selected within a group. Only data from the "on" radio button is sent when the form is submitted.

Attributes

%coreattrs, %i18n, %events, onblur, onfocus, onselect, onchange

checked
> Causes the radio button to be in the "on" state when the form is initially displayed.

name=text
> *Required.* Specifies the name of the control to be passed to the form-processing application if this element is selected.

value=text
> *Required.* Specifies the value of the parameter to be passed to the form-processing application.

<input type=reset>

`<input type=reset>` *(no end tag)*

NN 2, 3, 4, 6   MSIE 2, 3, 4, 5.5, 6   HTML 4.01   WebTV   Opera5

Creates a reset button that clears the contents of the elements in a form (or sets them to their default values).

Attributes

%coreattrs,   %i18n,   %events,   onblur,   onfocus,   onselect, onchange

value=*text*
> Specifies a value for the reset button control. This appears as the button label (it will say "Reset" by default).

<input type=submit>

`<input type=submit>` *(no end tag)*

NN 2, 3, 4, 6   MSIE 2, 3, 4, 5.5, 6   HTML 4.01   WebTV   Opera5

Creates a submit button control; pressing the button immediately sends the information in the form to the server for processing.

Attributes

%coreattrs,   %i18n,   %events,   onblur,   onfocus,   onselect, onchange

value=*text*
> Specifies a value for the submit button control. This appears as the button label (it will say "Submit" by default).

name=*text*
> *Required.* Specifies the name of this control to be passed to the form-processing application for this element.

<input type=text>

`<input type=text>` *(no end tag)*

NN 2, 3, 4, 6   MSIE 2, 3, 4, 5.5, 6   HTML 4.01   WebTV   Opera5

Creates a text input element. This is the default input type.

Attributes

%coreattrs,   %i18n,   %events,   onblur,   onfocus,   onselect, onchange `maxlength=number`

> Specifies the maximum number of characters the user can input for this element. The default is an unlimited number of characters.

`name=text`

> *Required.* Specifies the name for the text input control. This name will be sent, along with the value, to the form-processing application.

`size=number`

> Specifies the size of the text-entry box (measured in number of characters) to be displayed for this element. Users can type entries that are longer than the space provided, causing the field to scroll to the right.

`value=text`

> Specifies the value that will initially be displayed in the text box.

`<ins>`

<ins>...</ins>

NN 2, 3, 4, 6	MSIE 2, 3, 4, 5, 5.5, 6	HTML 4.01	WebTV	Opera5

Indicates text that has been inserted into the document. It has no inherent style qualities on its own but may be used to indicate inserted text in a different color via style sheet controls. It may be useful for legal documents and any instance in which edits need to be tracked. Its counterpart is deleted text (`<del>`). Both can be used to indicate either inline or block-level elements.

Attributes

`%coreattrs, %i18n, %events`

`cite=URL`

> Can be set to point to a source document that explains why the document was changed.

`datetime=YYYY-MM-DDThh:mm:ssTZD`

> Specifies the date and time the change was made. See `<del>` for an explanation of the date/time format.

<isindex>

NN 2, 3, 4, 6   **MSIE** 2, 3, 4, 5.5, 6   **HTML** 4.01   **WebTV**   **Opera5**

Deprecated. Marks the document as searchable. The server on which the document is located must have a search engine that supports this searching. The browser displays a text entry field and a generic line that says, "This is a searchable index. Enter search keywords." This method is outdated; more sophisticated searches can be handled with form elements and CGI scripting.

Attributes

%coreattrs, %i18n

<kbd>

NN 2, 3, 4, 6   **MSIE** 2, 3, 4, 5, 5.5, 6   **HTML** 4.01   **WebTV**   **Opera5**

Stands for "keyboard" and indicates text entered by the user. It is usually displayed in the browser's monospace font (usually Courier). Some browsers also display it in bold.

Attributes

%coreattrs, %i18n, %events

<label>

NN 2, 3, 4, 6   **MSIE** 2, 3, 4, 5.5, 6   **HTML** 4.01   WebTV   Opera5

Used to attach information to controls. Each label element is associated with exactly one form control.

Attributes

%coreattrs, %i18n, %events, onblur, onfocus

accesskey=*single character*
    Assigns an access key to the element. Pressing the access key gives focus to (jumps to and highlights) the element.

for=*text*
    Explicitly associates the label with the control by matching the value of the for attribute with the value of the id attribute within the control element.

Example

```
<LABEL for="lastname">Last Name: </LABEL>
<INPUT type="text" id="lastname" size="32">
```

<layer>   <layer>...</layer

NN 2, 3, **4**, 6   **MSIE** 2, 3, 4, 5, 5.5, 6   **HTML** 4.01   **WebTV**   **Opera5**

Identifies a layer in Navigator versions 4 through 4.7. Layers allow content elements to be exactly positioned, hidden, shown, stacked, or accessed by scripts. Netscape abandoned the <layer> and <ilayer> elements in Netscape 6 in favor of the standards-compliant <div> tag for similar functionality.

Attributes

above=*layer name*
> Specifies the name of the layer to be rendered above the current layer.

background=*URL*
> Specifies a background image for the layer.

below=*layer name*
> Specifies the name of the layer to be rendered below the current layer.

bgcolor=*#RRGGBB or color name*
> Specifies the color of the current layer.

class=*name*
> Gives the layer a class name to be referenced by a style sheet.

clip=*x,y,x,y*
> Indicates the visible area of the layer. Content outside the clipping area will be transparent. Its values are a pair of x,y coordinates indicating the top-left and bottom-right corners of the rectangle clipping path.

height=*number or %*
> Specifies the height of the layer.

id=*text*
> Gives the layer a unique identifying name for use with style sheets or scripts.

`left=`*`number`*

> Specifies the horizontal offset of a layer in pixels relative to its parent layer or the left page margin.

`name=`*`name`*

> Gives the layer a name that can be referenced by scripts. `id` can also be used.

`pagex=`*`number`*

> Specifies (in number of pixels) the horizontal position of the layer relative to the browser.

`pagey=`*`number`*

> Specifies (in number of pixels) the vertical position of the layer relative to the browser.

`src=`*`url`*

> Provides the location of a file to load into the layer.

`style=`*`style rules`*

> Specifies inline style information for the layer.

`top=`*`number`*

> Specifies (in number of pixels) the top offset of the layer, relative to its parent layer or the top page margin.

`visibility=hide|inherit|show`

> Indicates whether a layer is hidden, shown, or inherits its visibility from its parent layer.

`width=`*`number`*

> Specifies (in number of pixels) the width of the layer.

`zindex=`*`number`*

> Specifies a layer's stacking order relative to other layers. A value of 1 indicates the bottommost layer, with higher integers stacking above in order.

\<legend\>   `<legend>...</legend>`

NN 2, 3, 4, 6   **MSIE** 2, 3, **4, 5.5, 6**   **HTML** 4.01   WebTV   Opera5

Assigns a caption to a `<fieldset>` (it must be contained within a `<fieldset>` element). This improves accessibility when the `fieldset` is rendered nonvisually.

Attributes

%coreattrs, %i18n, %events

accesskey=*single character*
> Assigns an access key to the element. Pressing the access key gives focus to (jumps to and highlights) the element.

align=bottom | left | right | top
> *Deprecated.* Indicates the position of the legend relative to the <fieldset> element.

<li>

<li>...</li> *(end tag optional)*

NN 2, 3, 4, 6   MSIE 2, 3, 4, 5, 5.5, 6   HTML 4.01   WebTV   Opera5

Defines an item in a list. It is used within the <dir>, <ol>, and <ul> list tags.

Attributes

The following attributes have been deprecated by the HTML 4.0 specification in favor of style sheet controls for list item display.

%coreattrs, %i18n, %events

start=*number*
> *Deprecated.* Specifies the number for the first item in a numbered list.

type=*format*
> *Deprecated.* Changes the format of the automatically generated numbers or bullets for list items.
>
> Within unordered lists (<ul>), the type attribute can be used to specify the bullet style (disc, circle, or square) for a particular list item.
>
> Within ordered lists (<ol>), the type attribute specifies the numbering style (see the table in the <ol> entry) for a particular list item.

value=*number*
> *Deprecated.* Within ordered lists, you can specify the number of an item. Following list items increase from the specified number.

<link>

<link> *(no end tag)*

NN 2, 3, 4, 6   MSIE 2, 3, 4, 5, 5.5, 6   HTML 4.01   WebTV   Opera5

Defines a relationship between the current document and another document. This tag goes within the <head> portion of the document. It is often used to refer to an external style sheet.

Attributes

%coreattrs, %i18n, %events

charset=*character set id*
: Specifies the character set of the linked document.

href=*url*
: Identifies the target document.

hreflang=*language code*
: Identifies the language of the linked document.

media=screen|tty|tv|projection|handheld|print|braille| aural|all

Identifies the target medium for the linked document so an alternate style sheet can be accessed.

rel=*relation*
: Describes the relationship from the current source document to the target. Common relationship types include stylesheet, next, prev, copyright, index, and glossary.

rev=*relation*
: Specifies the relationship of the target document back to the source (the opposite of the rel attribute).

target=*frame or window name*
: Defines the frame or window name that will display the linked resource.

title=*text*
: Provides a title for the target document.

type=*resource*
: Shows the type of an outside link. The value text/css indicates that the linked document is an external cascading style sheet.

\<map\>

\<map\>...\</map\>

NN 2, 3, 4, 6	MSIE 2, 3, 4, 5, 5.5, 6	HTML 4.01	WebTV	Opera5

Encloses client-side imagemap specifications.

Attributes

%coreattrs, %i18n, %events

name=*text*
> *Required.* Gives the imagemap a name that is then referenced within the \<img\> tag.

\<marquee\>

\<marquee\>...\</marquee\>

NN 2, 3, 4, 6	**MSIE 2, 3, 4, 5, 5.5, 6**	HTML 4.01	**WebTV**	Opera5

Creates a scrolling-text marquee area.

Attributes

align=top|middle|bottom
> Aligns the marquee with the top, middle, or bottom of the neighboring text line.

behavior=scroll|slide|alternate
> Specifies how the text should behave. Scroll is the default setting and means the text should start completely off one side, scroll all the way across and completely off, then start over again. Slide stops the scroll when the text touches the other margin. Alternate means bounce back and forth within the marquee.

bgcolor=#*rrggbb* or *color name*
> Sets the background color of the marquee.

direction=left|right
> Defines the direction in which the text scrolls. IE 4.0+ also support the values up and down.

height=*number*
> Defines the height in pixels of the marquee area.

hspace=*number*
> Holds a number of pixels space clear to the left and right of the marquee.

`loop=`*`number`*`|infinite`

> Specifies the number of times the text loops as a number value or infinite.

`scrollamount=`*`number`*

> Sets the number of pixels to move the text for each scroll movement.

`scrolldelay=`*`number`*

> Specifies the delay, in milliseconds, between successive movements of the marquee text.

`vspace=`*`number`*

> Holds a number of pixels space clear above and below the marquee.

`width=`*`number`*

> Specifies the width in pixels of the marquee.

`<menu>`

<menu>...</menu>

NN 2, 3, 4, 6	MSIE 2, 3, 4, 5, 5.5, 6	HTML 4.01	WebTV	Opera5

Deprecated. This indicates the beginning and end of a menu list, which consists of list items `<li>`. Menus are intended to be used for a list of short choices, such as a menu of links to other documents. It is little used and has been deprecated in favor of `<ul>`.

Attributes

`%coreattrs, %i18n, %events`

`compact`

> Displays the list as small as possible (not many browsers do anything with this attribute).

`<meta>`

<meta> *(end tag forbidden)*

NN 2, 3, 4, 6	MSIE 2, 3, 4, 5, 5.5, 6	HTML 4.01	WebTV	Opera5

Provides additional information about the document. It should be placed within the `<head>` tags at the beginning of the document. It is commonly used for making documents searchable (by adding keywords) or to specify the character set for a document. Meta tags have been used for client-pull functions, but this function is discouraged.

Attributes

`%i18n`

`content=text`
> *Required.* Specifies the value of the meta tag property and is always used in conjunction with `name=` or `http-equiv=`.

`http-equiv=text`
> The specified information is treated as though it were included in the HTTP header that the server sends ahead of the document. It is used in conjunction with the `content` attribute (in place of the `name` attribute).

`name=text`
> Specifies a name for the meta information property.

`scheme=text`
> Provides additional information for the interpretation of meta data. This is a new attribute introduced in HTML 4.0.

`<multicol>`   `<multicol>...</multicol>`

NN 2, 3, 4, 6	MSIE 2, 3, 4, 5, 5.5, 6	HTML 4.01	WebTV	Opera5

Netscape 4.x only. Displays enclosed text in multiple columns of approximately the same length. It is rarely used.

Attributes

`cols=number`
> *Required.* Specifies the number of columns.

`gutter=number`
> Specifies the amount of space (in pixels) to maintain between columns.

`width=number`
> Specifies the width of the columns in pixels. All columns within `<multicol>` are the same width.

<nobr>
<nobr>...</nobr>

NN 2, 3, 4, 6   **MSIE 2, 3, 4, 5, 5.5, 6**   HTML 4.01   **WebTV**   **Opera5**

Nonstandard. Text (or graphics) within the "no break" tags always display on one line, without allowing any breaks. The line may run beyond the right edge of the browser window, requiring horizontal scrolling. The HTML 4.01 specification prefers style sheets for preventing line breaks.

<noembed>
<noembed>...</noembed>

NN 2, 3, 4, 6   **MSIE 2, 3, 4, 5, 5.5, 6**   HTML 4.01   **WebTV**   **Opera5**

The text or object specified by <noembed> appears when an embedded object cannot be displayed (e.g., when the appropriate plug-in is not available). This tag is placed within the <embed> container tags.

<noframes>
<noframes>...</noframes>

NN 2, 3, 4, 6   **MSIE 2, 3, 4, 5, 5.5, 6**   **HTML 4.01**   **WebTV**   **Opera5**

Defines content to be displayed by browsers that cannot display frames. Browsers that do support frames ignore the content between <noframes> tags.

Attributes

%coreattrs, %i18n, %events

<noscript>
<noscript>...</noscript>

NN 2, 3, 4, 6   **MSIE 2, 3, 4, 5, 5.5, 6**   **HTML 4.01**   **WebTV**   **Opera5**

Defines content to be displayed by browsers that do not support scripting or have scripting turned off.

Attributes

%coreattrs, %i18n, %events

NN 2, 3, 4, 6   **MSIE** 2, 3, 4, 5, 5.5, 6   **HTML** 4.01   **WebTV**   **Opera5**

A generic element used for placing an object (such as an image, applet, media file, etc.) on a web page. It is similar to the \<embed\> tag but is the W3C's approved method for adding elements to a page. Browser support for the \<object\> tag is not up to standards. Support in Navigator 4 is buggy, and in IE 4 (and even 5), the tag is generally useful only for ActiveX controls.

Attributes

%coreattrs, %i18n, %events

align=baseline|center|left|middle|right|textbottom|
textmiddle|texttop

> *Deprecated.* Aligns object with respect to surrounding text. See the \<img\> tag for explanations of the align values.

archive=*urls*

> Specifies a space-separated list of URLs for resources that are related to the object.

border=*number*

> *Nonstandard.* Sets the width of the border in pixels if the object is a link.

classid=*url*

> Identifies the location of an object's implementation. It is used with or in place of the data attribute. The syntax depends on the object type.

codebase=*url*

> Identifies the base URL used to resolve relative URLs in the object (similar to \<base\>). By default, the codebase is the base URL of the current document.

codetype=*codetype*

> Specifies the media type of the code. It is required only if the browser cannot determine an applet's MIME type from the classid attribute or if the server does not deliver the correct MIME type when downloading the object.

`data=url`
> Specifies the URL of the data used for the object. The syntax depends on the object.

`declare`
> *HTML 4.01.* Declares an object but restrains the browser from downloading and processing it. Used in conjunction with the `name` attribute, this facility is similar to a forward declaration in a more conventional programming language, letting you defer the download until the object actually gets used.

`height=number`
> Specifies the height of the object in pixels.

`hspace=number`
> *Deprecated.* Holds *number* pixels space clear to the left and right of the object.

`name=text`
> Specifies the name of the object to be referenced by scripts on the page.

`standby=message`
> *HTML 4.01.* Specifies the message to display during object loading.

`tabindex=number`
> Assigns the position of the current element in the tabbing order for the current document.

`type=type`
> Specifies the media type for the data.

`usemap=url`
> Specifies the imagemap to use with the object.

`vspace=number`
> *Deprecated.* Holds *number* pixels space clear above and below the object.

`width=number`
> Specifies the object width in pixels.

`<ol>`

NN 2, 3, 4, 6   MSIE 2, 3, 4, 5, 5.5, 6   HTML 4.01   WebTV   Opera5

Defines the beginning and end of an ordered (numbered) list, which consists of list items `<li>`. Item numbers are inserted automatically by the browser.

Attributes

%coreattrs, %i18n, %events

compact
> *Deprecated.* Displays the list as small as possible (not many browsers do anything with this attribute).

start=*number*
> Starts the numbering of the list at *number* instead of at 1.

type=1|A|a|I|i
> *Deprecated.* Defines the numbering system for the list as follows:

Type value	Generated style	Sample sequence
1	Arabic numerals (default)	1, 2, 3, 4
A	Uppercase letters	A, B, C, D
a	Lowercase letters	a, b, c, d
I	Uppercase Roman numerals	I, II, III, IV
i	Lowercase Roman numerals	i, ii, iii, iv

`<optgroup>`

NN 2, 3, 4, 6   MSIE 2, 3, 4, 5.5, 6   HTML 4.01   WebTV   Opera5

Defines a logical group of `<option>`s. This could be used by browsers to display hierarchical cascading menus. `<optgroups>` cannot be nested.

Attributes

%coreattrs, %i18n, %events

disabled
> Disables the form control.

label=*text*
>   *Required.* Specifies the label for the option group.

`<option>`

`<option>...</option>` *(end tag optional)*

NN 2, 3, 4, 6   MSIE 2, 3, 4, 5.5, 6   HTML 4.01   WebTV   Opera5

Defines an option within a select element (a multiple-choice menu or scrolling list). The end tag, although it exists, is usually omitted. The content of the `<option>` element is the value that is sent to the form processing application (unless an alternative value is specified using the value attribute).

Attributes

%coreattrs, %i18n, %events

disabled
>   Disables the form control.

label
>   Allows the author to provide a shorter label than the content of the option. This attribute is poorly supported.

selected
>   Makes this item selected when the form is initially displayed.

value=*text*
>   Defines a value to assign to the option item within the select control, to use in place of `<option>` contents.

`<p>`

`<p>...</p>` *(end tag optional)*

NN 2, 3, 4, 6   MSIE 2, 3, 4, 5, 5.5, 6   HTML 4.01   WebTV   Opera5

Denotes the beginning and end of a paragraph. While many browsers will also allow the `<p>` tag to be used without a closing tag to start a new paragraph, the container method is preferred. When using cascading style sheets with the document container, tags are required or the formatting will not work. Browsers ignore multiple empty `<p>` elements.

Attributes

%coreattrs, %i18n, %events

align=center|left|right
> *Deprecated.* Aligns the text within the tags to the left, right, or center of the page.

\<param\>   \<param\> *(no end tag)*

NN 2, 3, 4, 6	MSIE 2, 3, 4, 5, 5.5, 6	HTML 4.01	WebTV	Opera5

Supplies a parameter within the \<applet\> or \<object\> tag.

Attributes

id=*text*
> Gives the parameter a unique identifying name.

name=*text*
> *Required.* Defines the name of the parameter.

value=*text*
> Defines the value of the parameter.

valuetype=data|ref|object
> Indicates the type of value: data indicates that the parameter's value is data (default); ref indicates that the parameter's value is a URL; object indicates that the value is the URL of another object in the document.

type=*content type*
> *HTML 4.01.* Specifies the media type of the resource only when the valuetype attribute is set to ref. It describes the types of values found at the referred location.

\<pre\>   \<pre\>...\</pre\>

NN 2, 3, 4, 6	MSIE 2, 3, 4, 5, 5.5, 6	HTML 4.01	WebTV	Opera5

Delimits preformatted text, meaning that lines are displayed exactly as they are typed in, honoring multiple spaces and line breaks. Text within \<pre\> tags is displayed in a monospace font such as Courier.

Attributes

%coreattrs, %i18n, %events

width=*value*
> *Deprecated.* This optional attribute determines how many characters to fit on a single line within the <pre> block.

<q>
<q>...</q>

NN 2, 3, 4, **6**   **MSIE** 2, 3, **4, 5, 5.5, 6**   **HTML** 4.01   WebTV   **Opera5**

Delimits a short quotation that can be included inline, such as "to be or not to be." It differs from <blockquote>, which is for longer quotations set off as a separate paragraph element. Some browsers automatically insert quotation marks. When used with the lang (language) attribute, the browser may insert language-specific quotation marks.

Attributes

%coreattrs, %i18n, %events

cite=*url*
> Designates the source document from which the quotation was taken.

<rt>
<rt>...</rt>

NN 2, 3, 4, **6**   **MSIE** 2, 3, 4, **5, 5.5, 6**   **HTML** 4.01   WebTV   Opera5

Internet Explorer 5+ only. Indicates "ruby text," annotation or pronunciation guidelines that appear in small text above the base text. The <rt> element is used within the <ruby> element.

Attributes

%coreattrs, %i18n, %events

accesskey=*single character*
> Assigns an access key to the element. Pressing the access key gives focus to (jumps to and highlights) the element.

language=javascript|jscript|vbs|vbscript|xml
> Specifies the language that the current script is written in.

```
tabindex=number
```
Assigns the position of the current element in the tabbing order for the current document.

`<ruby>`

`<ruby>...</ruby>`

NN 2, 3, 4, 6	**MSIE** 2, 3, 4, **5, 5.5**, 6	HTML 4.01	WebTV	Opera5

Internet Explorer 5+ only. Identifies the base text that will be displayed with "ruby text" above. Ruby text can be used for special annotations or pronunciation guidelines.

Attributes

See the `<rt>` entry for a list of supported attributes.

Example

```
<ruby>This text will be used as the base text.
<rt>Ruby text appears in small text above the base text.
</rt>
</ruby>
```

`<s>`

`<s>...</s>`

NN 2, 3, 4, 6	**MSIE** 2, 3, **4, 5, 5.5, 6**	HTML 4.01	WebTV	Opera5

Deprecated. Enclosed text is displayed as strike-through text (same as `<strike>` but introduced by later browser versions).

Attributes

%coreattrs, %i18n, %events

`<samp>`

`<samp>...</samp>`

NN 2, 3, 4, 6	**MSIE** 2, 3, **4, 5, 5.5**, 6	HTML 4.01	WebTV	Opera5

Delimits sample output from programs, scripts, etc. Sample text is generally displayed in a monospace font.

Attributes

%coreattrs, %i18n, %events

<script>
<script>...</script>

NN 2, 3, 4, 6   MSIE 2, 3, 4, 5.5, 6   HTML 4.01   WebTV   Opera5

Places a script within the document. The script may be included in the document or loaded in from an external document.

Attributes

charset=*character set identifier*
Defines the character set of the linked resource.

defer
Indicates that the script does not generate any document content, so the user agent may continue parsing and rendering.

language=*scripting language name*
Deprecated. Identifies scripting language for the current script element. It has been deprecated in favor of type.

src=*url*
Provides location of external script.

type=*text*
Required. Identifies the scripting language of the current script element (for example, text/javascript) and overrides the default scripting language.

<select>
<select>...</select>

NN 2, 3, 4, 6   MSIE 2, 3, 4, 5.5, 6   HTML 4.01   WebTV   Opera5

Defines a multiple-choice menu or a scrolling list. It is a container for one or more <option> tags. This element may also contain one or more <optgroup>s.

Attributes

%coreattrs, %i18n, %events, onblur, onfocus, onchange

disabled
Disables the form element.

multiple
This allows the user to select more than one <option> from the list. When this attribute is absent, only single selections are allowed.

name=*text*

> Defines the name for select control; when the form is submitted to the form-processing application, this name is sent along with each selected option value.

size=*number*

> Specifies the number of rows that display in the list of options. For values higher than 1, the options are displayed as a scrolling list with the specified number of options visible. When size=1 is specified, the list is displayed as a pop-up menu.
>
> The default value is 1 when multiple is *not* used. When multiple is specified, the value varies by browser (but a value of 4 is common).

tabindex=*number*

> Assigns the position of the current element in the tabbing order for the current document.

`<small>`

`<small>...</small>`

NN 2, 3, 4, 6	MSIE 2, 3, 4, 5, 5.5, 6	HTML 4.01	WebTV	Opera5

Renders the type smaller than the surrounding text.

Attributes

%coreattrs, %i18n, %events

`<spacer>`

`<spacer>` *(no end tag)*

NN 2, 3, 4, 6	MSIE 2, 3, 4, 5, 5.5, 6	HTML 4.01	**WebTV**	Opera5

Holds a specified amount of blank space within the flow of a page. This is a proprietary tag introduced by Netscape; it met with controversy and is now rarely used in common practice. It can be used to maintain space within table cells for correct display in Navigator.

Attributes

align=*value*

> Aligns block spacer with surrounding text. Values are the same as for the `<img>` tag.

height=*number*
> Specifies height in number of pixels for a block spacer.

size=*number*
> Specifies a number of pixels to be used with a vertical or horizontal spacer.

type=vertical|horizontal|block
> Specifies the type of spacer: vertical inserts space between two lines of text, horizontal inserts space between characters, and block inserts a rectangular space.

width=*number*
> Specifies width in number of pixels for a block spacer.

\<span\>

...

NN 2, 3, 4, 6	MSIE 2, 3, 4, 5, 5.5, 6	HTML 4.01	WebTV	Opera5

Identifies a span of inline characters, but does not by default affect the formatting of those characters. It can be used in conjunction with the class and/or id attributes and formatted with cascading style sheets.

Attributes

%coreattrs, %i18n, %events

class=*name*
> Assigns a name to an element or a number of elements. Elements that share a class identification can be treated as a group.

id=*name*
> Assigns a unique name to an element. There may not be two elements with the same id name in a document.

style=*style properties*
> Embeds style information to be applied to the division contents.

`<strike>`

`<strike>...</strike>`

NN 2, 3, 4, 6	MSIE 2, 3, 4, 5, 5.5, 6	HTML 4.01	WebTV	Opera5

Deprecated. Enclosed text is displayed as strike-through text (crossed through with a horizontal line). The HTML 4.01 specification prefers style sheet controls for this effect.

Attributes

%coreattrs, %i18n, %events

`<strong>`

`<strong>...</strong>`

NN 2, 3, 4, 6	MSIE 2, 3, 4, 5, 5.5, 6	HTML 4.01	WebTV	Opera5

Enclosed text is strongly emphasized. Nearly all browsers render `<strong>` text in bold.

Attributes

%coreattrs, %i18n, %events

`<style>`

`<style>...</style>`

NN 2, 3, 4, 6	MSIE 2, 3, 4, 5, 5.5, 6	HTML 4.01	WebTV	Opera5

Allows authors to embed style sheet rules in the head of the document There may be any number of `<style>` elements in a document.

Attributes

%i18n

media=screen|tty|tv|projection|handheld|print|braille|
    aural|all

> Specifies the target medium to which the style sheet applies.

type=*content-type*

> *Required.* Specifies the style sheet language of the element's contents. The only viable type at this time is text/css.

title=*text*

> Provides a title for the element.

`<sub>`

`<sub>`...`</sub>`

NN 2, 3, 4, 6	MSIE 2, 3, 4, 5, 5.5, 6	HTML 4.01	WebTV	Opera5

Formats enclosed text as subscript.

Attributes

%coreattrs, %i18n, %events

`<sup>`

`<sup>`...`</sup>`

NN 2, 3, 4, 6	MSIE 2, 3, 4, 5, 5.5, 6	HTML 4.01	WebTV	Opera5

Formats enclosed text as superscript.

Attributes

%coreattrs, %i18n, %events

`<table>`

`<table>`...`</table>`

NN 2, 3, 4, 6	MSIE 2, 3, 4, 5, 5.5, 6	HTML 4.01	WebTV	Opera5

Defines the beginning and end of a table. The end tag is required, and its omission may cause the table not to render in some browsers.

Attributes

%coreattrs, %i18n, %events

align=left|right|center
> *Deprecated.* Aligns the table within the text flow (same as align in the `<img>` tag). The default alignment is left. The center value is not universally supported, so it is more reliable to center a table on a page using tags outside the table (such as `<center>` or `<div>`).

background=*url*
> *Nonstandard.* Specifies a graphic image to be tiled in the background of the table. In Internet Explorer 3.0 and higher, the image tiles behind the entire table. In Netscape Navigator 4.0, the tile repeats in each individual cell (although its support is not officially documented).

`bgcolor="#rrggbb"` *or* `color name`

Specifies a background color for the entire table. Value is specified in hexadecimal RGB values or by color name.

`border=`*number*

Specifies the width (in pixels) of the border around the table and its cells. Set it to `border=0` to turn the borders off completely. The default value is 1. Adding the word `border` without a value results in a 1-pixel border.

`cellpadding=`*number*

Sets the amount of space, in number of pixels, between the cell border and its contents. The default value is 1.

`cellspacing=`*number*

Sets the amount of space (in number of pixels) between table cells. The default value is 2.

`frame=void|above|below|hsides|lhs|rhs|vsides|box|border`

Tells the browser where to draw borders around the table. The values are as follows:

void	The frame does not appear (default)
above	Top side only
below	Bottom side only
hsides	Top and bottom sides only
vsides	Right and left sides only
lhs	Left side only
rhs	Right side only
box	All four sides
border	All four sides

When the `border` attribute is set to a value greater than zero, the frame defaults to `border` unless otherwise specified. This attribute was introduced by Internet Explorer 3.0 and now appears in the HTML 4.01 specification. Netscape supports this attribute in version 6 only.

`height=`*number, percentage*

Nonstandard. Specifies the minimum height of the entire table. It can be specified in a specific number of pixels or by a percentage of the parent element.

`hspace=`*`number`*

>Holds a number of pixels space to the left and right of a table positioned with the `align` attribute (same as `hspace` in the `<img>` tag).

`rules=all|cols|groups|none|rows`

>Tells the browser where to draw rules within the table. Its values are as follows:

none	No rules (default)
groups	Rules appear between row groups (thead, tfoot, and tbody) and column groups
rows	Rules appear between rows only
cols	Rules appear between columns only
all	Rules appear between all rows and columns

>When the `border` attribute is set to a value greater than zero, `rules` defaults to `all` unless otherwise specified.

>This attribute was introduced by Internet Explorer 3.0 and now appears in the HTML 4.01 specification. Netscape supports it in version 6 only.

`summary=`*`text`*

>Provides a summary of the table contents for use with nonvisual browsers.

`vspace=`*`number`*

>Holds a number of pixels space above and below a table positioned with the `align` attribute (same as `vspace` in the `<img>` tag).

`width=`*`number, percentage`*

>Specifies the width of the entire table. It can be specified in a specific number of pixels or by percentage of the parent element.

Internet Explorer only

`bordercolor="#`*`rrggbb`*`"` *`or color name`*

>Specifies the color of the main center portion of a table border. (Table borders are rendered using three color values to create a 3D effect.)

`bordercolorlight="#rrggbb"` or *color name*
  Specifies the color of the light shade used to render 3D-looking table borders.

`bordercolordark="#rrggbb"` or *color name*
  Specifies the color of the dark shade used to render 3D-looking table borders.

`<tbody>`   `<tbody>`...`</tbody>` *(start and end tags optional)*

NN 2, 3, 4, 6   **MSIE** 2, 3, 4, 5, 5.5, 6   **HTML** 4.01   WebTV   Opera5

Defines a row or group of rows as the "body" of the table. It must contain at least one row (`<tr>`).

"Row group" tags (`tbody`, `thead`, and `tfoot`) were introduced by Internet Explorer and are part of the HTML 4.01 specification. The attributes for `<tbody>` are currently not supported by any commercial browser. Row groups could speed table display and provide a mechanism for scrolling the body of a table independently of its head and foot. It could also be useful for printing long tables for which the head information could be printed on each page.

Attributes

`align=left|center|right|justify|char`
  Deprecated. Specifies horizontal alignment (or justification) of cell contents. The default value is `left`.

`char=character`
  Specifies a character along which the cell contents will be aligned. The default character is a decimal point (language-appropriate). This attribute is generally not supported by current browsers.

`charoff=length`
  Specifies the offset distance to the first alignment character (`char`) on each line. If a line doesn't use an alignment character, it should be horizontally shifted to end at the alignment position. This attribute is generally not supported by current browsers.

`valign=top|middle|bottom|baseline`
  Deprecated. Specifies vertical alignment of cell contents.

<td>

NN 2, 3, 4, 6   **MSIE** 2, 3, 4, 5, 5.5, 6   **HTML** 4.01   **WebTV**   **Opera5**

Defines a table data cell. The end tag is not required but may prevent unpredictable table display, particularly if the cell contains images. A table cell can contain any content, including another table.

Attributes

%coreattrs, %i18n, %events

align=left|center|right|justify|char
> *Deprecated.* Specifies horizontal alignment (or justification) of cell contents. The default value is left.

background=*url*
> Specifies a graphic image to be used as a tile within the cell. Netscape's documentation does not cover this tag, but it is supported by version 4.0.

bgcolor="#rrggbb" *or color name*
> Specifies a color to be used in the table cell. A cell's background color overrides colors specified at the row or table levels.

colspan=*number*
> Specifies the number of columns the current cell should span. The default value is 1. According to the HTML 4.01 specification, the value zero (0) means the current cell spans all columns from the current column to the last column in the table; in reality, however, this feature is not supported in current browsers.

height=*number, percentage*
> *Deprecated.* Specifies the height of the cell in number of pixels or by a percentage value relative to the table height. The height specified in the first column will apply to the rest of the cells in the row. The height values need to be consistent for cells in a particular row. Pixel measurements are more reliable than percentages, which only work when the height of the table is specified in pixels.

nowrap

> *Deprecated.* Disables automatic text wrapping for the current cell. Line breaks must be added with a `<br>` or by starting a new paragraph. This attribute is only supported in Internet Explorer 5 and higher.

rowspan=*number*

> Specifies the number of rows spanned by the current cell. The default value is 1. According to the HTML 4.01 specification, the value zero (0) means the current cell spans all rows from the current row to the last row; in reality, however, this feature is not supported by any browsers.

valign=top|middle|bottom|baseline

> *Deprecated.* Specifies the vertical alignment of the text (or other elements) within the table cell. The default is middle.

width=*number*

> *Deprecated.* Specifies the width of the cell in number of pixels or by a percentage value relative to the table width. The width specified in the first row will apply to the rest of the cells in the column, and the values need to be consistent for cells in the column.

Internet Explorer only

bordercolor="#*rrggbb*" *or color name*

> Defines the border color for the cell.

bordercolordark="#*rrggbb*" *or color name*

> Defines the dark shadow color for the cell border.

bordercolorlight="#*rrggbb*" *or color name*

> Defines the light highlight color of the cell border.

New in HTML 4.01

These attributes are part of the HTML standard but are not supported by current browsers.

abbr=*text*

> Provides an abbreviated form of the cell's content.

axis=*text*

> Places a cell into a conceptual category, which could then be used to organize or search the table in different ways.

char=character
> Specifies a character along which the cell contents will be aligned. The default character is a decimal point (language-appropriate).

charoff=length
> Specifies the offset distance to the first alignment character (char) on each line. If a line doesn't use an alignment character, it should be horizontally shifted to end at the alignment position.

headers=id reference
> Lists header cells (by id) that provide header information for the current data cell. This is intended to make tables more accessible to nonvisual browsers.

scope=row|col|rowgroup|colgroup
> Specifies the table cells for which the current cell provides header information. A value of col indicates that the current cell is the header for all the cells that fall below. colgroup indicates the current cell is the header for the column group that contains it. A value of row means that the current cell is the header for the cells in the rest of the row. rowgroup means the current cell is the header for the containing rowgroup. This is intended to make tables more accessible to nonvisual browsers.

<textarea>   `<textarea>...</textarea>`

NN 2, 3, 4, 6   **MSIE** 2, 3, 4, 5.5, 6   **HTML** 4.01   **WebTV**   **Opera5**

Defines a multiline text-entry control. The text that is enclosed within the <textarea> tags is displayed in the text-entry field when the form initially displays.

Attributes

%coreattrs, %i18n, %events, onblur, onfocus, onchange

accesskey=single character
> Assigns an access key to the element. Pressing the access key gives focus to (jumps to and highlights) the element.

cols=*number*
> *Required.* Specifies the visible width of the text-entry field, measured in number of characters. Users may enter text lines that are longer than the provided width, in which case the entry scrolls to the right (or wraps if the browser provides some mechanism for doing so).

disabled
> Disables the form element for user input.

name=*text*
> *Required.* Specifies a name for the text input control. This name will be sent along with the control content to the form-processing application.

rows=*number*
> *Required.* Specifies the height of the text-entry field in number of lines of text. If the user enters more lines than are visible, the text field scrolls down to accommodate the extra lines.

tabindex=*number*
> Assigns the position of the current element in the tabbing order for the current document.

wrap=off|virtual|physical
> *Nonstandard.* Sets word wrapping within the text area. off turns word wrapping off; users must enter their own line returns. virtual displays the wrap, but the line endings are not transmitted to the server. physical displays and transmits line endings to the server. Some browsers support the proprietary value soft as equivalent to virtual, and hard as equivalent to physical.

\<tfoot\>   \<tfoot\>...\</tfoot\> *(end tag optional)*

NN 2, 3, 4, 6   **MSIE** 2, 3, 4, 5, 5.5, 6   **HTML** 4.01   WebTV   Opera5

Defines the foot of a table and should contain information about a table's columns. It is one of the "row group" tags introduced by Internet Explorer and proposed in the HTML 4.01 specification. A \<tfoot\> must contain at least one row (\<tr\>).

See \<tbody\> for more information and a list of supported attributes.

`<th>`

`<th>...</th>` *(end tag optional)*

NN 2, 3, 4, 6   **MSIE** 2, 3, 4, 5, 5.5, 6   **HTML** 4.01   **WebTV**   **Opera5**

Defines a table header cell. Table header cells function the same as table data cells (`<td>`). Browsers generally display the content of table header cells in bold text centered horizontally and vertically in the cell (although some browsers vary). The end tag is optional.

Attributes

The `<th>` tag uses the same attributes as the `<td>` tag. See listing under `<td>`.

`<thead>`

`<thead>...</thead>` *(end tag optional)*

NN 2, 3, 4, 6   **MSIE** 2, 3, 4, 5, 5.5, 6   **HTML** 4.01   **WebTV**   **Opera5**

Defines the head of the table and should contain information about a table. It must contain at least one row (`<tr>`). `<thead>` is one of the "row group" tags introduced by Internet Explorer and proposed in the HTML 4.01 specification.

See `<tbody>` for more information and a list of supported attributes.

`<title>`

`<title>...</title>`

NN 2, 3, 4, 6   **MSIE** 2, 3, 4, 5, 5.5, 6   **HTML** 4.01   **WebTV**   **Opera5**

Required. Specifies the title of the document. The title generally appears in the top bar of the browser window. According to the HTML 4.01 specification, all documents must contain a meaningful `<title>` within the `<head>` of the document.

Attributes

`%i18n`

`<tr>`

`<tr>...</tr>` *(end tag optional)*

NN 2, 3, 4, 6   **MSIE** 2, 3, 4, 5, 5.5, 6   **HTML** 4.01   **WebTV**   **Opera5**

Defines a row of cells within a table. A table row as delimited by `<tr>` tags contains no content other than a collection of table cells

(`<td>`). Settings made in the `<tr>` tag apply to all the cells in that row, but individual cell settings override those made at the row level.

Attributes

%coreattrs, %i18n, %events

align=left|center|right|justify|char
> *Deprecated.* Aligns the text (or other elements) within the cells of the current row. This attribute has been deprecated by the HTML 4.01 specification in favor of positioning with style sheets.

bgcolor="#rrggbb" *or color name*
> Specifies a color to be used in the row. A row's background color overrides the color specified at the table level.

char=*character*
> Specifies a character along which the cell contents will be aligned. The default character is a decimal point (language-appropriate). This attribute is generally not supported by current browsers.

charoff=*length*
> Specifies the offset distance to the first alignment character (char) on each line. If a line doesn't use an alignment character, it should be horizontally shifted to end at the alignment position. This attribute is generally not supported by current browsers.

valign=top|middle|bottom|baseline
> *Deprecated.* Specifies the vertical alignment of the text (or other elements) within cells of the current row.

Internet Explorer only

background=*url of image file*
> Specifies a graphic image to be used as a tile within the row.

bordercolor="#rrggbb" *or color name*
> Defines the border color for the row.

bordercolordark="#rrggbb" *or color name*
> Defines the dark shadow color for the row border.

bordercolorlight="#rrggbb" or color name
  Defines the light highlight color of the row border.

<tt>

<tt>...</tt>

NN 2, 3, 4, 6   MSIE 2, 3, 4, 5, 5.5, 6   HTML 4.01   WebTV   Opera5

Formats enclosed text as teletype text. The text enclosed in the <tt> tag is generally displayed in a monospaced font such as Courier.

Attributes

%coreattrs, %i18n, %events

<u>

<u>...</u>

NN 2, 3, 4, 6   MSIE 2, 3, 4, 5, 5.5, 6   HTML 4.01   WebTV   Opera5

Deprecated. Enclosed text is underlined when displayed. The HTML 4.01 specification prefers style sheet controls for this effect.

Attributes

%coreattrs, %i18n, %events

<ul>

<ul>...</ul>

NN 2, 3, 4, 6   MSIE 2, 3, 4, 5, 5.5, 6   HTML 4.01   WebTV   Opera5

Defines the beginning and end of an unordered (bulleted) list, which consists of list items <li>. Bullets for each list item are inserted automatically by the browser.

Attributes

%coreattrs, %i18n, %events

compact
  Deprecated. Displays the list block as small as possible. Not many browsers support this attribute.

type=disc|circle|square
  Deprecated. Defines the shape of the bullets used for each list item.

<var>

<var>...</var>

NN 2, 3, 4, 6   **MSIE** 2, 3, 4, 5, 5.5, 6   **HTML** 4.01   **WebTV**   **Opera5**

Indicates an instance of a variable or program argument, usually displayed in italic.

Attributes

%coreattrs, %i18n, %events

<wbr>

<wbr>

NN 2, 3, 4, 6   **MSIE** 2, 3, 4, 5, 5.5, 6   HTML 4.01   WebTV   **Opera5**

Nonstandard. Indicates a potential word break point. The <wbr> tag works only when placed within <nobr>-tagged text and causes a line break only if the current line already extends beyond the browser's display window margins.

Character Entity Chart

Characters not found in the normal alphanumeric character set, such as © or &, must be specified in HTML using character entities. Character entities can be defined by name (&name;) or by numeric value (&#nnn;). The browser interprets the string to display the proper character. Named entities are preferable because numeric values may be interpreted differently on different platforms.

Unless otherwise noted, the character entities are part of the HTML 2.0 and later standards and will work with nearly all available browsers. An "N" in the description indicates that the character is a nonstandard entity.

Number	Name	Symbol	Description	Version
				Horizontal tab	

			Line feed	

			Carriage return	
 			Space	
!		!	Exclamation point	

Number	Name	Symbol	Description	Version
&#034;	&quot;	"cd /c	Quotation mark	
&#035;		#	Hash mark	
&#036;		$	Dollar symbol	
&#037;		%	Percent symbol	
&#038;	&amp;	&	Ampersand	
&#039;		'	Apostrophe (single quote)	
&#040;		(	Left parenthesis	
&#041;		)	Right parenthesis	
&#042;		*	Asterisk	
&#043;		+	Plus sign	
&#044;		,	Comma	
&#045;		-	Hyphen	
&#046;		.	Period	
&#047;		/	Slash	
0-9		0-9	Digits 0–9	
&#058;		:	Colon	
&#059;		;	Semicolon	
&#060;	&lt;	<	Less than	
&#061;		=	Equals sign	
&#062;	&gt;	>	Greater than	
&#063;		?	Question mark	
&#064;		@	Commercial at sign	
A-Z		A-Z	Letters A–Z	
&#091;		[	Left square bracket	
&#092;		\	Backslash	
&#093;		]	Right square bracket	
&#094;		^	Caret	
&#095;		_	Underscore	
&#096;		`	Grave accent (no letter)	

Number	Name	Symbol	Description	Version
a– z		a–z	Letters a–z	
&#123;		{	Left curly brace	
|		|	Vertical bar	
&#125;		}	Right curly brace	
&#126;		~	Tilde	
&#130;		‚	Low left single quote	N
&#131;		ƒ	Small f with hook	N
&#132;		„	Low left double quote	N
&#133;		…	Ellipsis	N
&#134;		†	Dagger	N
&#135;		‡	Double dagger	N
&#136;		ˆ	Circumflex	N
&#137;		‰	Per mille (per thousand)	N
&#138;		Š	Capital S, caron	N
&#139;		<	Less-than sign	N
&#140;		Œ	Capital OE ligature	N
&#145;		'	Left single curly quote	N
&#146;		'	Right single curly quote	N
&#147;		"	Left double curly quote	N
&#148;		"	Right double curly quote	N
&#149;		•	Bullet	N
&#150;		–	En dash	N
&#151;		—	Em dash	N
&#152;		~	Tilde	N
&#153;		™	Trademark	N
&#154;		š	Small s, caron	N
&#155;		>	Greater-than sign	N
&#156;		œ	Lowercase oe ligature	N
&#159;		Ÿ	Capital Y, umlaut	N
			Nonbreaking space	4.0

Number	Name	Symbol	Description	Version
&#161;	&iexcl;	¡	Inverted exclamation mark	4.0
&#162;	&cent;	¢	Cent sign	4.0
&#163;	&pound;	£	Pound symbol	4.0
&#164;	&curren;	¤	General currency symbol	4.0
&#165;	&yen;	¥	Yen symbol	4.0
&#166;	&brvbar;	¦	Broken vertical bar	4.0
&#167;	&sect;	§	Section sign	4.0
&#168;	&uml;	¨	Umlaut	4.0
&#169;	&copy;	©	Copyright	4.0
&#170;	&ordf;	ª	Feminine ordinal	4.0
&#171;	&laquo;	«	Left angle quote	4.0
&#172;	&not;	¬	Not sign	4.0
&#173;	&shy;		Soft hyphen	4.0
&#174;	&reg;	®	Registered trademark	4.0
&#175;	&macr;	¯	Macron accent	4.0
&#176;	&deg;	°	Degree sign	4.0
&#177;	&plusmn;	±	Plus or minus	4.0
&#178;	&sup2;	^{2}	Superscript 2	4.0
&#179;	&sup3;	^{3}	Superscript 3	4.0
&#180;	&acute;	´	Acute accent (no letter)	4.0
&#181;	&micro;	µ	Micron (Greek mu)	4.0
&#182;	&para;	¶	Paragraph sign	4.0
&#183;	&middot;	·	Middle dot	4.0
&#184;	&cedil;	¸	Cedilla	4.0
&#185;	&sup1;	^{1}	Superscript 1	4.0
&#186;	&ordm;	º	Masculine ordinal	4.0
&#187;	&raquo;	»	Right angle quote	4.0
&#188;	&frac14;	1/4	Fraction one-fourth	4.0
&#189;	&frac12;	1/2	Fraction one-half	4.0
&#190;	&frac34;	3/4	Fraction three-fourths	4.0

Number	Name	Symbol	Description	Version
¿	¿	¿	Inverted question mark	4.0
À	À	À	Capital A, grave accent	
Á	Á	Á	Capital A, acute accent	
Â	Â	Â	Capital A, circumflex accent	
Ã	Ã	Ã	Capital A, tilde accent	
Ä	Ä	Ä	Capital A, umlaut	
Å	Å	Å	Capital A, ring	
Æ	Æ	Æ	Capital AE ligature	
Ç	Ç	Ç	Capital C, cedilla	
È	È	È	Capital E, grave accent	
É	É	É	Capital E, acute accent	
Ê	Ê	Ê	Capital E, circumflex accent	
Ë	Ë	Ë	Capital E, umlaut	
Ì	Ì	Ì	Capital I, grave accent	
Í	Í	Í	Capital I, acute accent	
Î	Î	Î	Capital I, circumflex accent	
Ï	Ï	Ï	Capital I, umlaut	
Ð	Ð	Ð	Capital eth, Icelandic	
Ñ	Ñ	Ñ	Capital N, tilde	
Ò	Ò	Ò	Capital O, grave accent	
Ó	Ó	Ó	Capital O, acute accent	
Ô	Ô	Ô	Capital O, circumflex accent	
Õ	Õ	Õ	Capital O, tilde accent	
Ö	Ö	Ö	Capital O, umlaut	
×	×	×	Multiplication sign	4.0
Ø	Ø	Ø	Capital O, slash	
Ù	Ù	Ù	Capital U, grave accent	
Ú	Ú	Ú	Capital U, acute accent	
Û	Û	Û	Capital U, circumflex	
Ü	Ü	Ü	Capital U, umlaut	

Number	Name	Symbol	Description	Version
Ý	Ý	Ý	Capital Y, acute accent	
Þ	Þ	Þ	Capital Thorn, Icelandic	
ß	ß	ß	Small sz ligature, German	
à	à	à	Small a, grave accent	
á	á	á	Small a, acute accent	
â	â	â	Small a, circumflex accent	
ã	ã	ã	Small a, tilde	
ä	ä	ä	Small a, umlaut	
å	å	å	Small a, ring	
æ	æ	æ	Small ae ligature	
ç	ç	ç	Small c, cedilla	
è	è	è	Small e, grave accent	
é	é	é	Small e, acute accent	
ê	ê	ê	Small e, circumflex accent	
ë	ë	ë	Small e, umlaut accent	
ì	ì	ì	Small i, grave accent	
í	í	í	Small i, acute accent	
î	î	î	Small i, circumflex accent	
ï	ï	ï	Small i, umlaut	
ð	ð	ð	Small eth, Icelandic	
ñ	ñ	ñ	Small n, tilde	
ò	ò	ò	Small o, grave accent	
ó	ó	ó	Small o, acute accent	
ô	ô	ô	Small o, circumflex accent	
õ	õ	õ	Small o, tilde	
ö	ö	ö	Small o, umlaut	
÷	÷	÷	Division sign	4.0
ø	ø	ø	Small o, slash	
ù	ù	ù	Small u, grave accent	
ú	ú	ú	Small u, acute accent	

Number	Name	Symbol	Description	Version
û	û	û	Small u, circumflex accent	
ü	ü	ü	Small u, umlaut	
ý	ý	ý	Small y, acute accent	
þ	þ	þ	Small thorn, Icelandic	
ÿ	ÿ	ÿ	Small y, umlaut	

Extended HTML 4.01 Entities

The HTML 4.01 specification introduces a wide variety of new character entities for rendering foreign languages, mathematical material, and other symbols. Their support is limited to the latest browser versions (IE 5.5 and NN 6, although NN4.x supports the Latin Extended-A set).

Latin Extended-A

Number	Name	Symbol	Description	Version
Œ	Œ	Œ	Capital ligature OE	4.0
œ	œ	œ	Small ligature oe	4.0
Š	Š	Š	Capital S, caron	4.0
š	š	š	Small s, caron	4.0
&#376	Ÿ	Ÿ	Capital Y, umlaut	4.0

Latin Extended-B

Number	Name	Symbol	Description	Version
ƒ	ƒ	ƒ	Small f with hook	4.0

Spacing Modifier Letters

Number	Name	Symbol	Description	Version
ˆ	ˆ	^	Circumflex accent	4.0

Number	Name	Symbol	Description	Version
˜	˜	~	Tilde	4.0

Greek

Number	Name	Symbol	Description	Version
Α	Α	A	Greek capital alpha	4.0
Β	Β	B	Greek capital beta	4.0
Γ	Γ	Γ	Greek capital gamma	4.0
Δ	Δ	Δ	Greek capital delta	4.0
Ε	Ε	E	Greek capital epsilon	4.0
Ζ	Ζ	Z	Greek capital zeta	4.0
&#919	Η	H	Greek capital eta	4.0
Θ	Θ	Θ	Greek capital theta	4.0
Ι	Ι	I	Greek capital iota	4.0
Κ	Κ	K	Greek capital kappa	4.0
Λ	Λ	Λ	Greek capital lambda	4.0
Μ	Μ	M	Greek capital mu	4.0
Ν	Ν	N	Greek capital nu	4.0
Ξ	Ξ	Ξ	Greek capital xi	4.0
Ο	Ο	O	Greek capital omicron	4.0
Π	Π	Π	Greek capital pi	4.0
Ρ	Ρ	P	Greek capital rho	4.0
Σ	Σ	Σ	Greek capital sigma	4.0
Τ	Τ	T	Greek capital tau	4.0
Υ	Υ	Y	Greek capital upsilon	4.0
Φ	Φ	Φ	Greek capital phi	4.0
Χ	Χ	X	Greek capital chi	4.0
Ψ	Ψ	Ψ	Greek capital psi	4.0
Ω	Ω	Ω	Greek small omega	4.0
α	α	α	Greek small alpha	4.0
β	β	β	Greek small beta	4.0

Number	Name	Symbol	Description	Version
&#947;	&gamma;	γ	Greek small gamma	4.0
&#948;	&delta;	δ	Greek small delta	4.0
&#949;	&epsilon;	ε	Greek small epsilon	4.0
&#950;	&zeta;	ζ	Greek small zeta	4.0
&#951;	&eta;	η	Greek small eta	4.0
&#952;	&theta;	θ	Greek small theta	4.0
&#953;	&iota;	ι	Greek small iota	4.0
&#954;	&kappa;	κ	Greek small kappa	4.0
&#955;	&lambda;	λ	Greek small lambda	4.0
&#956;	&mu;	μ	Greek small mu	4.0
&#957;	&nu;	ν	Greek small nu	4.0
&#958;	&xi;	ξ	Greek small xi	4.0
&#959;	&omicron;	o	Greek small omicron	4.0
&#960;	&pi;	π	Greek small pi	4.0
&#961;	&rho;	ρ	Greek small rho	4.0
&#962;	&sigmaf;	ς	Greek small letter final sigma	4.0
&#963;	&sigma;	σ	Greek small sigma	4.0
&#964;	&tau;	τ	Greek small tau	4.0
&#965;	&upsilon;	υ	Greek small upsilon	4.0
&#966;	&phi;	φ	Greek small phi	4.0
&#967;	&chi;	χ	Greek small chi	4.0
&#968;	&psi;	ψ	Greek small psi	4.0
&#969;	&omega;	ω	Greek small omega	4.0
&#977;	&thetasym;	ϑ	Greek small theta symbol	4.0
&#978;	&upsih;	ϒ	Greek upsilon with hook	4.0
&#982;	&piv;	ϖ	Greek pi symbol	4.0

General Punctuation

Number	Name	Symbol	Description	Version
			En space	4.0
			Em space	4.0
			Thin space	4.0
&#8204;	&zwnj;	Non-printing	Zero-width non-joiner	4.0
&#8205;	&zwj;	Non-printing	Zero-width joiner	4.0
&#8206;	&lrm;	Non-printing	Left-to-right mark	4.0
&#8207	&rlm;	Non-printing	Right-to-left mark	4.0
&#8211;	&ndash;	–	En dash	4.0
&#8212;	&mdash;	—	Em dash	4.0
&#8216;	&lsquo;	'	Left single quotation mark	4.0
&#8217;	&rsquo;	'	Right single quotation mark	4.0
&#8218;	&sbquo;	‚	Single low-9 quotation mark	4.0
&#8220;	&ldquo;	"	Left double quotation mark	4.0
&#8221;	&rdquo;	"	Right double quotation mark	4.0
&#8222;	&bdquo;	„	Double low-9 quotation mark	4.0
&#8224;	&dagger;	†	Dagger	4.0
&#8225;	&Dagger;	‡	Double dagger	4.0
&#8226;	&bull;	•	Bullet	4.0
&#8230;	&hellep;	...	Ellipses	4.0
&#8240;	&permil;	‰	Per mille symbol (per thousand)	4.0
&#8242;	&prime;	′	Prime, minutes, feet	4.0
&#8243;	&Prime;	″	Double prime, seconds, inches	4.0
&#8249;	&lsaquo;	‹	Single left angle quotation *(nonstandard)*	4.0
&#8250;	&rsaquo;	›	Single right angle quotation *(nonstandard)*	4.0

Number	Name	Symbol	Description	Version
‾	‾	‾	Overline	4.0
⁄	⁄	/	Fraction slash	4.0
€	€	€	Euro symbol	4.0

Letter-like Symbols

Number	Name	Symbol	Description	Version
℘	℘	℘	Script capital P, power set	4.0
ℑ	ℑ	ℑ	Blackletter capital I, imaginary part	4.0
ℜ	ℜ	ℜ	Blackletter capital R, real part	4.0
™	™	™	Trademark sign	4.0
ℵ	ℵ	ℵ	Alef symbol, or first transfinite cardinal	4.0

Arrows

Number	Name	Symbol	Description	Version
←	←	←	Left arrow	4.0
↑	↑	↑	Up arrow	4.0
→	→	→	Right arrow	4.0
↓	↓	↓	Down arrow	4.0
↔	↔	↔	Left-right arrow	4.0
↵	↵	↵	Down arrow with corner leftwards	4.0
⇐	⇐	⇐	Leftwards double arrow	4.0
⇑	⇑	⇑	Upwards double arrow	4.0
⇒	⇒	⇒	Rightwards double arrow	4.0
⇓	⇓	⇓	Downwards double arrow	4.0
⇔	⇔	⇔	Left-right double arrow	4.0

Mathematical Operators

Number	Name	Symbol	Description	Version
∀	∀	∀	For all	4.0
∂	∂	∂	Partial differential	4.0
∃	∃	∃	There exists	4.0
∅	∅	∅	Empty set, null set, diameter	4.0
∇	∇	∇	Nabla, backward difference	4.0
∈	∈	∈	Element of	4.0
&#8713	∉	∉	Not an element of	4.0
∋	∋	∋	Contains as a member	4.0
∏	∏	Π	N-ary product, product sign	4.0
∑	∑	Σ	N-ary summation	4.0
−	−	−	Minus sign	4.0
∗	∗	*	Asterisk operator	4.0
√	√	√	Square root, radical sign	4.0
∝	∝	∝	Proportional	4.0
∞	∞	∞	Infinity symbol	4.0
∠	∠	∠	Angle	4.0
∧	∧	∧	Logical and, wedge	4.0
∨	∨	∨	Logical or, vee	4.0
∩	∩	∩	Intersection, cap	4.0
∪	∪	∪	Union, cup	4.0
∫	∫	∫	Integral	4.0
∴	∴	∴	Therefore	4.0
∼	∼	~	Tilde operator, varies with, similar to	4.0
≅	≅	≅	Approximately equal to	4.0
≈	≈	≈	Almost equal to, asymptotic to	4.0
≠	≠	≠	Not equal to	4.0
≡	≡	≡	Identical to	4.0

Number	Name	Symbol	Description	Version
≤	≤	≤	Less than or equal to	4.0
≥	≥	≥	Greater than or equal to	4.0
⊂	⊂	⊂	Subset of	4.0
⊃	⊃	⊃	Superset of	4.0
⊄	⊄	⊄	Not a subset of	4.0
⊆	&sube	⊆	Subset of or equal to	4.0
⊇	&supe	⊇	Superset of or equal to	4.0
⊕	⊕	⊕	Circled plus, direct sum	4.0
⊗	⊗	⊗	Circled times, vector product	4.0
⊥	⊥	⊥	Up tack, orthogonal to, perpendicular	4.0
⋅	⋅	·	Dot operator	4.0

Miscellaneous Technical Symbols

Number	Name	Symbol	Description	Version
⌈	⌈	⌈	Left ceiling	4.0
⌉	⌉	⌉	Right ceiling	4.0
⌊	⌊	⌊	Left floor	4.0
⌋	&rfloor	⌋	Right floor	4.0
〈	⟨	〈	Left-pointing angle bracket	4.0
〉	⟩	〉	Right-pointing angle bracket	4.0

Geometric Shapes

Number	Name	Symbol	Description	Version
◊	◊	◊	Lozenge	4.0

Miscellaneous Symbols

Number	Name	Symbol	Description	Version
♠	♠	♠	Black spade suit	4.0
♣	&clubs	♣	Black club suit	4.0
♥	♥	♥	Black heart suit	4.0
♦	&diams	♦	Black diamond suit	4.0

Decimal to Hexadecimal Conversion Chart

dec = hex	dec = hex	dec = hex	dec = hex	dec = hex	dec = hex
0 = 00	43 = 2B	86 = 56	129 = 81	172 = AC	215 = D7
1 = 01	44 = 2C	87 = 57	130 = 82	173 = AD	216 = D8
2 = 02	45 = 2D	88 = 58	131 = 83	174 = AE	217 = D9
3 = 03	46 = 2E	89 = 59	132 = 84	175 = AF	218 = DA
4 = 04	47 = 2F	90 = 5A	133 = 85	176 = B0	219 = DB
5 = 05	48 = 30	91 = 5B	134 = 86	177 = B1	220 = DC
6 = 06	49 = 31	92 = 5C	135 = 87	178 = B2	221 = DD
7 = 07	50 = 32	93 = 5D	136 = 88	179 = B3	222 = DE
8 = 08	51 = 33	94 = 5E	137 = 89	180 = B4	223 = DF
9 = 09	52 = 34	95 = 5F	138 = 8A	181 = B5	224 = E0
10 = 0A	53 = 35	96 = 60	139 = 8B	182 = B6	225 = E1
11 = 0B	54 = 36	97 = 61	140 = 8C	183 = B7	226 = E2
12 = 0C	55 = 37	98 = 62	141 = 8D	184 = B8	227 = E3
13 = 0D	56 = 38	99 = 63	142 = 8E	185 = B9	228 = E4
14 = 0E	57 = 39	100 = 64	143 = 8F	186 = BA	229 = E5
15 = 0F	58 = 3A	101 = 65	144 = 90	187 = BB	230 = E6
16 = 10	59 = 3B	102 = 66	145 = 91	188 = BC	231 = E7
17 = 11	60 = 3C	103 = 67	146 = 92	189 = BD	232 = E8
18 = 12	61 = 3D	104 = 68	147 = 93	190 = BE	233 = E9
19 = 13	62 = 3E	105 = 69	148 = 94	191 = BF	234 = EA
20 = 14	63 = 3F	106 = 6A	149 = 95	192 = C0	235 = EB
21 = 15	64 = 40	107 = 6B	150 = 96	193 = C1	236 = EC
22 = 16	65 = 41	108 = 6C	151 = 97	194 = C2	237 = ED
23 = 17	66 = 42	109 = 6D	152 = 98	195 = C3	238 = EE
24 = 18	67 = 43	110 = 6E	153 = 99	196 = C4	239 = EF
25 = 19	68 = 44	111 = 6F	154 = 9A	197 = C5	240 = F0
26 = 1A	69 = 45	112 = 70	155 = 9B	198 = C6	241 = F1
27 = 1B	70 = 46	113 = 71	156 = 9C	199 = C7	242 = F2
28 = 1C	71 = 47	114 = 72	157 = 9D	200 = C8	243 = F3
29 = 1D	72 = 48	115 = 73	158 = 9E	201 = C9	244 = F4
30 = 1E	73 = 49	116 = 74	159 = 9F	202 = CA	245 = F5
31 = 1F	74 = 4A	117 = 75	160 = A0	203 = CB	246 = F6
32 = 20	75 = 4B	118 = 76	161 = A1	204 = CC	247 = F7
33 = 21	76 = 4C	119 = 77	162 = A2	205 = CD	248 = F8
34 = 22	77 = 4D	120 = 78	163 = A3	206 = CE	249 = F9
35 = 23	78 = 4E	121 = 79	164 = A4	207 = CF	250 = FA
36 = 24	79 = 4F	122 = 7A	165 = A5	208 = D0	251 = FB
37 = 25	80 = 50	123 = 7B	166 = A6	209 = D1	252 = FC
38 = 26	81 = 51	124 = 7C	167 = A7	210 = D2	253 = FD
39 = 27	82 = 52	125 = 7D	168 = A8	211 = D3	254 = FE
40 = 28	83 = 53	126 = 7E	169 = A9	212 = D4	255 = FF
41 = 29	84 = 54	127 = 7F	170 = AA	213 = D5	
42 = 2A	85 = 55	128 = 80	171 = AB	214 = D6	

Other Titles Available from O'Reilly

Web Authoring and Design

HTML & XHTML: The Definitive Guide, 5th Edition

By Chuck Musciano & Bill Kennedy
5th Edition August 2002
672 pages, ISBN 0-596-00382-X

Our new edition offers web developers a better way to become HTML-fluent, by covering the language syntax, semantics, and variations in detail and demonstrating the difference between good and bad usage. Packed with examples, *HTML & XHTML: The Definitive Guide*, 5th Edition covers Netscape Navigator 6, Internet Explorer 6, HTML 4.01, XHTML 1.0, JavaScript 1.5, CSS2, Layers, and all of the features supported by the popular web browsers.

Learning Web Design

By Jennifer Niederst
1st Edition March 2001
418 pages, ISBN 0-596-00036-7

In *Learning Web Design*, Jennifer Niederst shares the knowledge she's gained from years of experience as both web designer and teacher. She starts from the very beginning—defining the Internet, the Web, browsers, and URLs—assuming no previous knowledge of how the Web works. Jennifer helps you build the solid foundation in HTML, graphics, and design principles that you need for crafting effective web pages.

Cascading Style Sheets: The Definitive Guide

By Eric A. Meyer
1st Edition May 2000
470 pages, ISBN 1-56592-622-6

CSS is the HTML 4.0–approved method for controlling visual presentation on web pages. *Cascading Style Sheets: The Definitive Guide* offers a complete, detailed review of CSS1 properties and other aspects of CSS1. Each property is explored individually in detail with discussion of how each interacts with other properties. There is also information on how to avoid common mistakes in interpretation. This book is the first major title to cover CSS in a way that acknowledges and describes current browser support, instead of simply describing the way things work in theory. It offers both advanced and novice web authors a comprehensive guide to implementation of CSS.

Perl for Web Site Management

By John Callender
1st Edition October 2001
528 pages, ISBN 1-56592-647-1

Perl for Web Site Management shows readers how to use Perl to help do everyday web tasks. Assuming no prior programming experience, this book teaches how to write CGI scripts, incorporate search engines, convert multiple text files into HTML, monitor log files, and track users as they navigate to a site. Whether the reader is a web programmer, web administrator, a designer—or simply a dabbler, this book provides a practical, hands-on introduction to Perl.

SVG Essentials

By J. David Eisenberg
1st Edition, February 2002
368 pages, ISBN 0-596-00223-8

SVG Essentials shows developers how to take advantage of SVG's open text-based format. Although SVG is much more approachable than the binary or PostScript files that have dominated graphics formats so far, developers need a roadmap to get started creating and processing SVG files. This book provides an introduction and reference to the foundations developers need to use SVG, and demonstrates techniques for generating SVG from other XML formats.

Dreamweaver MX: The Missing Manual

By David McFarland
1st Edition November 2002
792 pages, ISBN 0-596-00349-8

Dreamweaver MX: The Missing Manual is the ideal companion to this complex software. The book begins with an anatomical tour of a web page, and then walks users through the process of creating and designing a complete web site. Armed with this book, both first-time and experienced web designers can easily use Dreamweaver to bring stunning, interactive web sites to life. In addition, users new to database-driven web sites will be given an overview of the technology and a brief primer on using this new functionality in Dreamweaver.

Building Data-Driven Web Sites with Dreamweaver MX

By Simon Allardice
1st Edition May 2003 (est.)
376 pages (est.), ISBN 0-596-00340-4

The book teaches power users, step by step, how to create web pages with Dreamweaver MX (formerly UltraDev) that access a remote database using ColdFusion, ASP, ASP .Net, JSP, or PHP—without a lot of programming. Readers will benefit from the author's first-hand knowledge and polished teaching style.